PRAISE FOR

Rich20Something

"*Rich20Something* reminded me that my goals aren't too far off, and that, regardless of my age, I can create a business that gives me freedom and great income!"
—Arne Giske, founder, *The Millennial Entrepreneur* podcast

"Daniel DiPiazza gives you all the tools to build the foundation for your dreams to become a reality."
—Bruce Rodrigues de Jesus, entrepreneur

"I always knew I wanted to do something big but it wasn't until I became part of Daniel's community and started learning from him that I actually took action. Thanks to him and Rich20Something .com for inspiring and motivating me every day!"
—Jordan Nicole Gill, founder, Jordan and Janes

"Daniel is a truly down-to-earth person who doesn't mind getting in the trenches with you. . . . I have seen my life—and business— grow tremendously due to the valuable knowledge I've obtained as part of the Rich20Something community."
—Andre Hill, CEO and award-winning producer

"Daniel's support with the Rich20Something community and his insights are probably the #1 reason I've had the success I've experience in business so far."
—Robert James Collier, founder, Entrepreneurs Dinner

"I could have gained so much from this book earlier in my career. . . . DiPiazza does a great job helping readers figure out what their most marketable skills are and how to build a business around those skills and interests. In a word, this book is actionable."
—Jeremy Goldman, founder and CEO, Firebrand Group

"Irreverent millennial DiPiazza has a unique voice and a comprehensive strategy for twentysomethings to 'level up' and become entrepreneurs, including, but not limited to, building and growing an online business and working a side hustle. Perfect for those who are just getting into the tech game and need some inspirational leadership, *Rich20Something* will definitely help you build a business you care about."

—*Forbes*, "13 Must-Read Entrepreneurial Books for Tech Leaders"

"At its core, *Rich20Something* destroys some of the 'requirements' that I faced as a young adult finding my way to my career. . . . I feel like I'll be a better father and mentor for it all."

—*Huffington Post*

RICH
20SOMETHING

Ditch Your Average Job,

Start an Epic Business,

and Score the Life You Want

DANIEL DIPIAZZA

A TarcherPerigee Book

tarcherperigee

An imprint of Penguin Random House LLC
375 Hudson Street
New York, New York 10014

Most TarcherPerigee books are available at special quantity discounts for
bulk purchase for sales promotions, premiums, fund-raising, and
educational needs. Special books or book excerpts also can be created to
fit specific needs. For details, write: SpecialMarkets@
penguinrandomhouse.com.

ISBN 9780143129387 (hardcover)
ISBN 9780143129394 (paperback)

Printed in the United States of America
10   9   8   7   6   5   4   3   2   1

For my grandmother, Dana Wade.

I wish you were here to see this book come to life. It would have never happened without your love and guidance for the last twenty-eight years. Damn it, I miss you!

I was so looking forward to cracking open this book at Barnes & Noble with you. I can see you with your little hot chocolate now, sipping diligently as you read.

You told me once that your biggest dream was to go back to school and get a degree in creative writing. I hope this work makes you proud.

I wish we had more time together.

You made me a better person and, most importantly, you made me laugh. You definitely weren't a "normal" grandmother. You were my best friend, my confidant, and my #1 fan.

Thank you, thank you, thank you. A million times, thank you.

I love you and I'll never forget you. I promise to carry on the work that you never got to finish.

Contents

Introduction

I CAN REMEMBER VERY clearly now the precise moment my mind underwent "the shift." I was in the back of the kitchen at LongHorn Steakhouse in Atlanta, scooping little clumps of butter into those round plastic containers so that people would have something fatty to slather all over their massive basket of ciabatta bread. Mmm, delicious!

My manager, Scott, walked up behind me and peered over my shoulder. *"Do it again. Those balls look like shit."*

"Balls?" I asked, looking down at my pants to make sure I wasn't exposed.

"Those butter balls. Rescoop them. They look like they were scooped by some kid on the short bus. You're wasting point-zero-zero-seven micrograms of butter per day with those uneven portions. That's probably costing us fifty dollars per year. Do you want to give me fifty dollars?"

What I wanted to give him was five hundred punches right in the face.

In reality, though, that type of nit-picking by management happened every day. It was nothing special. But that day . . . something very different happened in my brain. A light went on (or perhaps several lights), and a very strong voice filled my head with a potent question: *Why are you wasting your potential at this job that means nothing to you, around these people who don't inspire you?*

And for the first time in my life, I was speechless . . . I couldn't even answer myself. **I knew I had to get out—and from that day forward, I became literally obsessed with figuring out this whole "making money" thing.**

Why did some people struggle their entire lives just to make ends meet, while others got to live carte blanche with enough money and resources to do whatever they wanted? Was there really a correlation between formal education and success, as I'd been told my entire life? Or was there some other X factor at play?

These are the things I wanted to know desperately—and I set out to find the answers, even if it meant making an embarrassing failure of myself. After all, I'd already scooped butter balls for a living. It's all up from there, right?

FAST-FORWARD A FEW YEARS to June 14, 2011. It was a Tuesday. I practically exploded into my apartment, opening the door with so much force that the doorknob dented the wall. My confidence was at about a trillion percent. From the outside, it was just an ordinary day. But inside, I was on fire.

I could have dunked on LeBron James from half-court on that day. I could have beaten Usain Bolt off the line by a mile.

In my gorilla grip, I clutched one of those thick manila envelopes—you know, the kind with the little metal prong on the flap.

Inside, the envelope was STACKED with dozens of checks bearing my name—and crisp hundred-dollar bills, with the big faces. There was over ten thousand dollars in there. And it was all mine.

I walked into the bedroom. My girlfriend, Sara, was watching TV. I grabbed the remote and turned it off without asking. (I'll admit, I was feeling a little cocky.) Then I flicked open that flimsy metal clasp on the envelope and dumped the contents on the bed.

"OK, now let's spread that shit out and roll on it," I said.

I'm sure you can guess what happened next, and I'm intentionally censoring the rest of the story in case my mom ever actually reads this.

I CALL THAT LITTLE STORY my "Scarface moment," in homage to Pacino's character when he got his first taste of the good life—and yes, I know it's a bit over the top. Yet almost five years later, I still can't stop thinking about that moment. Why?

Well, for one, I'd just made ten thousand dollars in about five hours of work. (Yep, you read that right.) But more than the change in my bank balance, that moment catalyzed a powerful and permanent change in my outlook on life.

On that fateful day, I realized that I no longer had to settle for just "getting by." *Now I was in control.* Never again would I have to play the "spray and pray" career game, throwing my résumé in with a sea of one thousand other recent grads, hoping that someone would hire me. And I sure as hell never had to work a job that I hated for less money than I deserved.

Maybe you're reading this and scoffing. Young people are supposed to do jobs they don't like initially. It builds character, some say. Not me, though. I could never stand spending a single minute doing something that didn't interest me. And I'd finally realized that just because generations before me had struggled through years of low-paying drudgery to claw their way up the ladder—so they could inflict the same misery on the next generation—did not mean I had to play into that game.

Is this the same jaded or "entitled" millennial outlook that the media has been saying for years will be my generation's downfall? Maybe. But guess what? I took a gamble and *I was right*. And over the past three years, I've taught hundreds of thousands of eager twentysomethings how to break the shackles of their nine-to-fives and use their skills to start businesses of their own.

Our generation eschews the idea that you must "pay your dues." We'd rather hack the system and get results faster. We reject society's opinion of us as entitled. We know our strengths . . . and we know that we're hungry for success. But with many of the old-school systems and career fields crumbling around us, it's time to find another path.

Or blaze a new one of our own.

Who Is *Rich20Something* For?

In just a few years, I'd gone from working at a restaurant and making $2.17 an hour (plus tips) to launching one, then two, then THREE successful businesses—a test prep agency, a web design firm, and a consulting company—and scaling them all to more than a hundred thousand dollars with no start-up capital. A few years after that, I took my skills online and made my first million by starting Rich20Something and teaching young people how to escape the nine-to-five trap.

How did I do it? Did I come up with the next Google or get a loan from a rich uncle? Hell no. I simply learned how to take skills I already had and create products and services that people would pay me money for. But it gets even better.

As my first few freelance businesses grew, I decided to write a series of articles and open letters detailing my experiences and frustrations with the nine-to-five struggle. My complaints were simple: I wanted to do work that made me feel alive. I was sick of working long hours for robotic bosses who saw me as a cog in a wheel. And dammit, I wanted to get paid well. Not because I felt entitled, but because it's hard—especially these days—to make a decent living that will help you afford the basics in life, let alone more important things like having a family or saving for retirement. Life is expensive.

Turns out that lots of other people all over the world felt the same way. I didn't think my writing was particularly revolutionary or insightful, but thousands of shares and comments poured in, to the point where I accidentally broke the Internet. Oops.

What stood out to me most was how many readers said they'd been struggling with the exact same things—suffering in silence, thinking they were alone—including:

- College students and recent graduates who didn't know what they wanted . . . but knew the traditional career path wasn't for them
- Employees in corporate careers or office jobs that didn't inspire them, who desperately wanted to leave their nine-to-five gigs and live their dreams on their own terms, but who didn't have a clue about where or how to get started
- Good, smart people who were overstressed, overworked, and underpaid—and looking for a path to personal, professional, and financial freedom

If any of these describes you, then the book you have in your hands could change everything. Starting now. I'm beyond pumped to have this opportunity to share my work with the world—not because I want to stroke my own ego with two hundred pages of "me-centric" rants, but because I know that what I've learned over the past few years about business and life can help you get from where you are to where you want to be. And I'll show you how.

How to Use This Book

This book contains all the tools you'll need to radically improve your career and life and power through the limiting beliefs that are holding you back from achieving your goals.

As you might expect, I'll teach you how to start and grow a business that you care about. You'll make money—that's a fact. But you'll also learn how to think about the world in a way that will allow you to see all the opportunities around you that were previously hidden.

I've designed this book to be easily digested, to be a guide that can be thumbed through, browsed, and read in any particular order that you see fit. It follows my own story in a loosely chronological format, but each chapter also stands alone. Take what you need and implement it.

Throughout the material, you'll notice that I've tied a lot of the actionable advice into examples drawn from all kinds of fields, from business to philosophy to history. My goal is to show you that there's more than one way to get the job done. This isn't a paint-by-numbers how-to manual where you must follow each step and piece of advice exactly to get the career you want. Think of it more like a recipe for general career success, where you can make your own decisions about how much of each ingredient to add to get the results you want. I think it's best that way because it gives you the flexibility to take control of your future and make it what you want on your terms.

I've included everything that I've needed to learn in order to pull myself up by my bootstraps, build businesses that I care about, achieve professional and financial success, and live an epic life like the ones most of us dream about. But a book on just my story and my advice would be boring and not helpful. So I've taken it one step further and included in-depth perspectives at the end of most of the chapters from other entrepreneurs, hustlers, and hackers from all different industries who are absolutely killing the game. Some of them are in their twenties. Some are in their sixties. Some are in the beginning stages but absolutely crushing it. Some are multi-multimillionaires who've been around the block. I don't discriminate. What you'll find is that they all share common threads in their outlook on the world. **They all wanted more and weren't afraid to take it!**

I dug deep with them and asked a ton of questions, among them things like:

- What's your why?
- What's the most important thing you had to sacrifice to get here?
- What was your biggest excuse that you had to overcome?
- What's something you never thought you'd have to know . . . that ended up being crucial to your success?
- What's something about who you are that has massively contributed to your success?
- What's the one piece of advice you'd go back and say to yourself on the day you started your business?

Do yourself a favor: Do NOT skip these case studies. They are not "filler" material. They are an integral part of understanding the mind-set, strategies, and tactics you'll need to take your career and your life to the next level. And they are vital in understanding how each person's path to success is different. If they can do it, so can you!

Finally, to supplement your learning and help you fast-track your success, I've put together a ton of bonuses for you, including all new videos, free downloads, and other resources to dive even deeper into the strategies you'll be learning here. **You can get that all for free at www.Rich20Something.com /bonus.**

Most importantly, have fun as you read this, but remember that the real fun (and the tough part) comes when you put the book down and start taking action. I'll be rooting for you!

Now let's get started!

PART I

The Struggle

The Three New Truths That Will Help You Break Free of the Nine-to-Five Slog

THE WORLD ISN'T just changing. It has already changed. Just a few decades ago, the path to the "good life" seemed so obvious. Go to school. Graduate college. Pay your dues. Build your career. Just play by the rules and you'd be guaranteed a spot at the table. That's what we were promised by our parents, our grandparents, our teachers and professors, our politicians, and our society as a whole. But look around you. Those promises have been broken. That system is broken, and there's no fixing it.

It's time to start recognizing the game being played around you. The rules have changed. In fact, there are no more rules that you know you can follow to find guaranteed success. So it's time to start standing up for what you really want, instead of settling for the scraps society tosses at you and barely getting by. It's time to unlock your true potential.

But how? The first step is awareness. If something feels "off" in your life, that's because something IS off. If you're dissatisfied, uninspired, or in pain, don't just hide your feelings and hope that they go away. They won't. They'll only intensify!

If you're unhappy with where your life is headed, if you're looking for a big breakthrough to show you where you should go next, if you're ready to make a change but just don't know how to take the first step, I can tell you one thing for sure: You won't find any more clarity by continuously "trying on" lives that don't fit you, hoping to find a match.

You have to create something entirely unique. Entirely you. In order to do that, you must first learn what I call the **Three New Truths.**

You No Longer Have to Pay Your Dues

(NEW TRUTH #1)

*You do not have to pass through point B to travel
from point A to point C.* — *Jace Hall*

KEY TAKEAWAYS

$ In today's world, the hustle isn't about "working your way up the ladder"; it's about creatively leveraging your skills to get to the top more quickly.

$ You will piss some people off when you skip steps. And that's OK.

$ You must let go of the idea that you have to "pay your dues" before you "deserve" success.

WHEN I MADE IT to Atlanta in 2010, I was looking for anybody and everybody with a little bit more life experience than me to lend some insight into what I should be doing with my life—and how to make it happen.

So I did what any other twenty-two-year-old would do: I went on Facebook. Not because I really thought I'd find a mentor there, but probably because I was bored. As luck would have it, I ran across Jace Hall.

Jace was everything I wanted to be in fifteen years. He's a video game, television, and film producer with some impressive credits. He's in incredible shape. Dates a famous fitness model. But he's also a nerd. Down-to-earth and accessible. And from what I could see, he'd figured out the whole "making money" thing.

On a whim, I decided to email him and ask for some advice about how I could become "successful." What he told me changed the way I looked at the world, and from then on, his simple advice has operated as a guiding principle in my life.

I've copied the email conversation here for you to read.

Subject: What the hell . . . why not?

Jace,

My name is Daniel, and I'm a twenty-one-year-old actor/ writer in Atlanta.

I don't know you personally, but you know how social networking goes. One person knows somebody, everybody knows somebody. I didn't even know you existed until a few weeks ago on Facebook.

I saw your info, I thought, OK, this guy is some big shot producer, supermodel girlfriend . . . he's probably so far removed from this planet it's not even funny.

But the more I looked into you, your show (pretty funny, by the way), and what you're about, the more I realized you are refreshingly average. Borderline dorky, and I mean that in the kindest way. You're not afraid to be who you are.

This was pretty exciting to me because it got me thinking—

if this guy can pull himself from wherever he was to where he is now, anybody can do it. You're pretty inspiring, because in you, I see my own potential.

I was hoping you could shed some light on your career and how you got to where you are today. Mentality, strokes of luck, or strokes of genius . . . I just want to know what it took.

Thanks for your time—talk soon,

Daniel DiPiazza

www.DanielDiPiazza.com

As I read through this conversation again after many years, I'm simultaneously smiling and cringing. On one hand, I recognize that this email exchange was a crucial step in my growth, and I'm grateful for Jace's generosity in replying to me. On the other hand, my approach to the conversation sounds like so many of the rambling emails that I get nowadays, and I wonder, *How could I have been so naive, to think he would care to help me, a stranger, out?*

Well, as you can tell, I was HUNGRY! I won't go deeper into criticizing the content of this email, because the point is, I had the balls to try.

A word to the wise, though: I'm not recommending you start emailing all the successful people you know for vague, general career advice like I did here. Asking successful people to "shed some light on your career" is asking for a LOT, especially via email and especially when you don't have a previous relationship with them. Can you imagine asking Michael Phelps to shed some light on how he became the most decorated Olympic athlete of all time?

"Ah, yes, it all started when my parents met in 1984!"

Way too general! It's just not a good question to email people who are in constant demand. The best move here would be to really research the people by yourself first and, once you've learned everything about them that you can, ask a more specific question that they can answer directly. Over time, if you build a relationship with these people, you may earn more in-depth responses from them. Still, Jace was gracious and gave me the nugget I'd been looking for—even though I didn't recognize it right away.

His response:

Daniel,

Thank you for your kind words. They are appreciated!

In regard to your question, for the moment there is no way that I have enough time to give you a thorough rundown on everything.

So instead, I will just give you a quote from a book that captures the level of determination you need to have. I think of it often . . .

"He piled upon the whale's white hump the sum of all the general rage and hate felt by his whole race . . . and then, as if his chest had been a mortar, he burst his hot heart's shell upon it."

Everyone will tell you no. Everyone will say that you can't. ALWAYS.

You must never believe it. It is not true. There are no rules. There is no spoon. The most determined player ALWAYS wins.

Just know this: YOU DO NOT HAVE TO PASS THROUGH
POINT B TO TRAVEL FROM POINT A TO POINT C.
Trust me.

Hope your day is great!

Jace

His words struck me like a lightning bolt: *You do not have to pass through point B to travel from point A to point C.* Still, I wrestled with the idea in my mind for weeks afterward. I understood it intuitively, but wasn't quite sure how to apply it to my life at the time. Little did I know that this insight would turn out to be a driving force in my life for the next decade.

A Generation of Hackers

Your parents and grandparents are going to hate hearing this, but it's true: **You no longer have to pay your dues.**

At least not in the traditional sense. The old approach to climbing the success ladder was focused on time spent playing the corporate game. The education system is the foundation for this model. Go to college for four years and get a bachelor's, and then you'll get a basic job. Spend two more years and get a master's, you'll get a slightly better job. Or want to really go the extra mile and potentially make some money? Try four more years at medical school, followed by another four years of residency! All the suffering in the process—the time and money spent, the boredom and exhausting hardships endured—that is your "dues." Didn't your grandfather ever tell you how he had to walk to school uphill both ways in the snow? No, the world wasn't shaped differently back then. He's talking about paying those dues, baby!

In the old model, you're not supposed to be able to progress to the next level without paying your dues. **And you're damn sure not supposed to ask questions.** You will have to suffer for long periods of time, doing millions of things that you don't like, to have a shot at getting what you want out of life. And even then, there are no guarantees.

Everybody knew this fact and had begrudgingly accepted it. Until now. Sometime in the early 2000s during the dotcom tech explosion, the system began to change. Young people became more impatient with the sluggish pace at which their lives were progressing versus the speed of their technology, knowledge, and skills. They wanted more, they wanted it now, and the technology was evolving just fast enough to meet their demands.

People like Alex Tew showed up at the right place at precisely the right time, and his efforts with the Million Dollar Homepage are a prime example of eschewing the "climb the ladder" approach and embracing creativity and hustle.

John Romaniello on How to Hustle

My solution to pretty much everything is just to work more. That's how I built my personal trainer business. When I got more clients, I didn't make them wait; I just started earlier and finished later. I do that because, although I've transitioned from personal training, I want to work until I die. I want to die right after I've typed the last period of something I'm writing; I want to die right there in the chair. I never want to retire. Why would I? Someone asking me when I want to retire, why I don't just retire now—that means we can't be friends. Our values are just too different.

Teddy Roosevelt got shot in the chest just before a speech . . . and he still did the speech. A ninety-minute speech, by the way. That's the attitude I have, and that's the attitude I need my friends to have.

You need to be around people who have the same values you do. Who believe that you're going to succeed. Who assume you're going to succeed. Because a very high level of belief is needed from yourself if you want to succeed, and so you can't have anyone around you who doesn't have that too.

John Romaniello

New York Times *best-selling author of* Engineering the Alpha

www.RomanFitnessSystems.com

The Million Dollar Homepage:
How to Make $1,037,100 in Five Months

Alex Tew didn't give a damn about paying his dues.

At twenty-one, he was about to start a three-year business management course at the University of Nottingham, but there was one small problem: money. He didn't want to be saddled with ridiculous student loan debt that would take years to pay off. While most students his age would have just shrugged and accepted the fact that society "required" them to play by the rules, Alex's mind was in a completely different place.

He started brainstorming fund-raising ideas that would help him make some extra income to pay off the loans quickly, and decided to launch a basic website that would sell one million pixels on the homepage to advertisers for one dollar each. A truly strange idea in 2005 that has since been copied ad nauseam.

Tew is originally from England, but thought that the idea of "million dollar" was more attractive than "million pound" from a marketing perspective. There are more Americans online as well, so he decided to go with US currency. For the record, I think he was right!

The pixels, which are too hard to see individually, would be sold in blocks of ten by ten. The minimum purchase was one hundred dollars. Each advertiser could choose what pictures they wanted to display in their allotted space and to which sites they wanted the pixels to link. The plan was ingeniously simple, but Alex had no idea if it would actually work.

He remarked on FT.com:

From the outset I knew the idea had potential, but it was one of those things that could have gone either way. My thinking was, I had nothing to lose (apart from the fifty euros or so it cost to register the domain and set up the hosting). I knew that the idea was quirky enough to create interest . . . The internet is a very powerful medium.

The Million Dollar Homepage opened up shop on August 26, 2005.

The first few sales rolled in slowly—mostly to family and friends—propelled entirely by word of mouth. But after more people started to hear about the site, word spread more quickly. The BBC picked up the story, and it blew up. Visitors poured in. Advertisers lined up. After only one month, the site had made over $250,000. After two months, over $500,000.

Demand spiked around New Year's in 2006, and only one thousand pixels were left. In the interest of fairness, Tew auctioned the remaining slots off on eBay to the tune of $38,100. He'd just made $1,037,100 in five months. Media attention was largely positive, calling the idea a brilliant example of novel, innovative advertising and entrepreneurship in the Internet age.

Naturally, others were less enthused. Don Oldenburg of the *Washington Post* called the site "cheap" and "mind-bogglingly lucrative," a "marketing monstrosity" and an "advertising badlands of spam, banner ads and pop-ups."

He went on to say:

> It looks like a bulletin board on designer steroids, an advertising train wreck you can't not look at. . . . It's like getting every pop-up ad you ever got in your life, at once. It's the Internet equivalent of suddenly feeling like you want to take a shower.

Commentary like this always makes me laugh because it's a PRIME example of how deeply ingrained the pay your dues mentality runs in many of us.

Oldenburg (perhaps appropriately named?) seems to imply that Tew doesn't "deserve" such praise or reward because the Million Dollar Homepage doesn't follow procedure. It's way outside the box. It's ugly.

At the very root of his complaint, he probably feels like Alex's success wasn't earned. And I get where he's coming from. To witness a stupid, simple website like this make more in five months than most traditional employees make in an entire career might be infuriating and mind-boggling to some.

It triggers the same type of rage you feel when you see an invention on late-night TV and think to yourself, *I could have thought of that!* I've been there. The urge to give in to jealousy and envy is strong. But to the hackers, misfits, and rebels of our generation, these types of massive wins by the underdogs of society are simply validation that we're on the right path.

Their success means that we can do the same. *You are part of this new world, and the opportunity to make such massive strides is yours as well as Alex's.*

Am I telling you to go out and build another Million Dollar Homepage? Of course not. It probably wouldn't work. The allure was in the novelty. What you should be paying attention to is Alex's trajectory and overall approach to creating his life. His willingness to take risks. His rejection of the "time spent" model and his playful approach to ethically skipping steps and getting ahead. This is how you need to start thinking.

I will teach you how, but first you must be open to the idea. Just like Jace Hall told me years ago, you don't need to pass through point B to move from point A to point C. With creativity and hustle, you can live the life of your dreams now. Not in thirty years.

Oh, by the way: After the success of the Million Dollar Homepage, Alex dropped out of the business degree he was fund-raising for in the first place. And not a single due was paid. Take that, establishment.

Quick Recap

There is a new truth for you to accept, and it is this: You do not have to pass through point B to get from point A to point C. Paying your dues, something your parents had to do, something your grandparents had to do— that age is over. And lots of parents and grandparents won't like this new truth. Even some of your friends won't like it, because if you don't have to pay your dues, that means you can be successful NOW. And that's scary to a lot of people.

It's pointless to think this isn't true, because people like Alex Tew prove it every single day. He built a simple website, advertised it, and made over one million dollars in five months. No dues paid whatsoever. If anybody convinces you to let go of this antiquated mind-set, let it be Alex.

Notes from the Field

Nathan Chan, CEO and Publisher of *Foundr* Magazine

Nathan is one of my closest friends, and he lives a world away in Melbourne, Australia. We connected a few years ago when we both had no audience to speak of—and literally no idea what we were doing. But just like high school classmates, we came up through the ranks and passed the tests of entrepreneurship together.

He's driven *Foundr* to the absolute top of the game, and it's now the number one digital magazine for entrepreneurs in the world. I couldn't be happier to call him a friend.

Check out the amazing community he's built at www .FoundrMagazine.com.

The work I do with Foundr *is what I was born to do. I'm good at it. I know I can build a company. And I want to show people what's possible through the world of entrepreneurship; I want them to know that they don't have to do shit they hate, or what you're told to do, or what your family wants you to do.*

I've sacrificed a few things. First, time. I've spent so many hours grinding behind the scenes, doing stuff that people will never see. I've sacrificed my reputation, because you have to be prepared to not give a shit about what anyone else thinks of you—even, and especially, if you're failing. I've even sacrificed some health: I stopped going to the gym because I wanted to spend as much time and energy on Foundr *as possible. Though I'm finally getting back to working out now.*

I would absolutely do it all over again, because I'm happier than I've ever been, I'm doing the work I was born to do, I'm having fun, I'm getting paid, I have an amazing team, and I get to speak to the most successful business-people in the world and hack their brains. Life is amazing. I have the best job ever, because it's one I created.

The most difficult part of the journey, and when I came closest to giving up, was when I was sued for trademark infringement. The lesson here: Don't call your business a name similar to something else. Do your research!

I persisted because I didn't want to let people down. As long as we had one paid subscriber, I was going to keep going. Not letting people down is extremely impor-tant to me, which I actually only realized when I started Foundr. *Not wanting to let people down has forced me to keep learning, to build an incredible shipping engine, and to just care about my customers.*

I didn't start my journey earlier because I didn't have a lot of confidence in my own abilities. I didn't do well at high school, or at university, or at my nine-to-five job. I never achieved much in those places, so I definitely didn't have the confidence to do something I really wanted to do. The only reason I started at all was because the frus-tration of my nine-to-five was bigger than my fear of starting my own company.

Being successful, to me, means living a good life: hav-

ing happy relationships, living my dream, doing work that fulfills me, getting financially rewarded—although money is the least important of those.

The first thing I think someone should do when starting a business is to find a mentor. Find someone who's done what you're trying to do, so you can learn from his or her mistakes instead of making your own.

Something that people need to start a business that they might not know they need is resourcefulness. If things aren't working out, you have to be able to find a solution, somehow, through persisting. The most important thing an entrepreneur can do is care. Never think about the customer as someone who pays you, and always think about how you can provide epic services that solve the customer's problems.

Something that's helped me to be successful is my obsessive personality. I wanted this business to work and I was obsessive about making it work, and I believe that's the only way to build a successful business.

2

The Game Has Changed—and You Can Make Your Own Rules

(NEW TRUTH #2)

You have to understand, most of these people are not ready to be unplugged. And many of them are so inert—so hopelessly dependent on the system—that they will fight to protect it.
—Morpheus
  The Matrix

KEY TAKEAWAYS:

$ You can hate or resent people for being successful, or you can become one of them.

$ You don't need to go to college to make an impact on the world. You just need Wi-Fi, a laptop, and a lot of coffee.

$ The longer you stay in school, the bigger your loans get and the more money you end up giving the government. So it's in the government's interest to keep you in college.

> **$** There are so many exciting alternatives to college, and one of them might even lead to you finding your "life's work."

BLEEEEEP! BLEEEEEP! BLEEEEEP!

It's seven fifteen in the morning and your iPhone is screaming at you to wake up. But you've already been up for ten minutes with your eyes closed, dreading the inevitable. In your mind, just one question: *Do I really have to do this AGAIN?*

The answer is implied. You kill the alarm and fight the urge to roll over and hit "snooze." What's another nine minutes? Let's just get this over with. Another Monday and you're going through the motions as usual. Get dressed in the dark. Go to work. Do your job. Try not to piss anybody off. Fake smile.

Some days are busy. Your boss needs things from you. Your coworkers need things from you. You try to cram down a chicken salad sandwich during your forty-five-minute lunch break. Other days, you spend your time toggling between tabs of Facebook and Gmail, trying to appear just busy enough to avoid having your work ethic questioned. As it turns out, there's a science to fucking around the whole day while still appearing occupied.

You get home exhausted. *Dancing with the Stars* is on. You zone out and wait for sleep to hit.

Tomorrow, more of the same. Days like this string together into weeks, months, and sometimes years.

You look up every once in a while: *How is it Christmas already?*

But every so often, you detect a tiny "glitch" in the system. Kinda like in *The Matrix*, when Neo walks through a crowd of sober worker bees all dressed in black and spots an elegant blonde in a red cocktail dress. The effect is jarring. These "glitches" stand out like a sore thumb.

Maybe you're reading *Forbes* and catch a glimpse of some young, brilliant entrepreneur in her twenties who's making billions with an app she developed in her dorm room. Glitch. Or perhaps it's the newest junior executive at your job, who, despite being with the company for less time than you, has already put himself on track to become a partner. Meanwhile, your boss just rejected your request for a raise. Glitch.

These seemingly extraordinary people pop up on social media too. How many times have you had to look at friends of friends taking selfies from Fiji as you agonize over which formula to use in an Excel spreadsheet? It just doesn't seem fair.

Who ARE these people, and what are they doing that I'm not?

It's easy to look at outstanding people doing incredible things and think of them as outliers. They must just be freaks of nature—not "one of us." Unusually gifted. Uncharacteristically lucky. Probably have rich parents. Born with better facial structure. Ugh. The unfairness would be depressing if it wasn't so intriguing.

At the end of the day, you can come up with all sorts of reasons why the "chosen few" should see massive success while you sit on the sidelines, fighting for the scraps with the rest of the population. You can even choose to hate them because of their success.

Or you could simply decide to become one of them.

The Invisible Game Being Played Around You

There's a game being played around you every single day, and whether or not you know the rules, you're a player. There's a reason why a special few seem to experience financial overflow and make millions while most of us are just "grateful to have a job in this economy."

There's a reason why a handful of people seem to always be traveling the world, eating incredible foods, or getting tickets to events that you didn't even know existed. It's all part of this invisible game.

In the Middle Ages, winners of the game were determined by power and violence. If you could kill more people than the other guy, you got to be king (until someone killed you—see *Game of Thrones*). Over time, politics and money shaped the rules of the game even more. We saw dynasties and monopolies determine who had the power, from the Rockefellers to the Kennedys.

And while some of these elements are still factors in 2017, there's now an even more powerful tool to play the game with—and it doesn't require money, power, or connections. In fact, it's available to everyone, regardless of where you start.

That tool is knowledge.

In 2017, if you have a skill or ability that you can use to help somebody else, you can make six (or seven) figures just by sharing that information and helping people solve their problems. No worries—I'll explain exactly how to find and develop these skills later. But before I do that, let's take a second to think more critically about this invisible game that society has forced us to play—and how you can bend the rules a little to come out on top.

Repeat after me: *College is dead.*

Somebody from a "really good family" just read that, closed the book, and proceeded to have palpitations. Stay with me while I explain.

I have no idea where my bachelor's degree is. I think it's in a storage unit by my old house in Florida. I never took it out of the flimsy envelope they mailed it in. Since World War II, American youth have been conditioned to believe that the best way to "make something of yourself"—and to ensure your financial success—is to go to college.

This is what we're taught in school. This is what our parents tell us. This is what we see on TV and in movies. It's part of our culture.

The old formula: A four-year college degree = happiness and a steady paycheck.

But look around you. Can you honestly say that this holds true anymore? When you look at the world's most successful people, formal education isn't always a common denominator. If anything, dropping out of college may be more common (see Mark Zuckerberg and Steve Jobs).

The common thread among the world's smartest, most successful people isn't their ability to play nicely within the system, check off everything on the syllabus, or maintain a perfect 4.0 GPA. Their incredible impact on the world wasn't a result of them working their way up somebody else's ladder.

The things they all have in common are their abilities to think outside the box, believe in themselves when others don't, and, above all, hustle hard. I remember walking into the guidance counselor's office the first week of undergrad and attempting to pick out my major. What a ridiculous exercise.

She swiveled around her computer screen from the opposite side of her desk to reveal a list of about 112 different specializations, listed in alphabetical order from accounting to zoology. In a separate pamphlet on her desk, there was a complete listing of the approximate "starting salaries" for graduates of each major. *Eighty-five thousand dollars for computer science? Ah, now I see why everyone wants to start programming . . .*

It seemed like a fun game to play: Match the major that sounds bearable with the salary you'd like to make. Kind of like *Deal or No Deal* for careers. Simple enough. Until it dawned on me: *Oh shit. Whatever I pick today I have to STICK with. For years.*

That was a major problem. At eighteen, I couldn't even be depended on to finish an entire book, let alone years of dedicated study in a field that I didn't even know anything about yet. How could I be expected to chart my path this early?

This is the part of the invisible game that's in place to trap us early in our development. By design, the university system is a money machine that goads us into making decisions before we're presented with all the information—or worse yet, one that encourages us to choose our studies based on how much money a degree in that field might make us.

These are horrible ways to make such an important, life-changing decision, and they often lead us to make choices that don't reflect what we actually want in the long run. Remember: Because of the outrageous, ever-increasing cost of tuition and the relative ease of getting student loans, it actually benefits the school, the government, and the banks for you to make uninformed decisions that keep you studying (and paying) for longer. Damn.

The longer you stay in school trying to "find your path," the more money you spend on tuition and the longer you pay off student loan debt to the government and the banks.

Somewhere in a secluded mansion, a Mr. Monopoly look-alike is cackling with delight as he sips champagne and counts every single dollar you spent switching your career focus from premed to criminology to communication.

Here's the reality: The invisible game being played around us is set up to make the traditional path of *school* ➡ *more school* ➡ *career* ➡ *retire* seem like the only possible route to happiness and security.

I'm here to tell you unreservedly that you no longer need college in order to be successful in life. You no longer need a university degree to find meaningful work that pays you what you deserve. In fact, going the traditional route may even hinder this process more than help it.

Today, the world thrives on ambitious, smart risk-takers who know how to make things happen for themselves and, most importantly, solve problems for other people. You don't need a degree to teach you this. You won't learn this by sitting in a lecture hall with four hundred other people.

Some of the best examples of these ambitious risk-takers are featured in the case studies contained in this book. As I mentioned before: Don't skip these sections!

You can change the world with Wi-Fi and a strong cup of coffee, no college required.

What to Do Instead of Going to College (or After You've Already Gone)

If I had to do it all over again, I would skip the university route and instead spend three to four years working on a kick-ass, meaningful project that could actually make an impact on the world. You end up learning WAY more this way than by sitting in a classroom, and it'll be about a hundred thousand dollars cheaper.

More importantly, by deeply involving yourself in things that you really care about, you'll start gaining real, experiential knowledge. This is the type of knowledge that you just can't get by going to class.

To be clear, I'm not anti-college; I'm pro-options. Many of us aren't even aware that there is a way to find work that you love that doesn't involve browsing through a catalog of majors and sitting in a lecture hall. Even if you read this and still choose to go to college, you should actively look to improve your life and intentionally develop yourself by undertaking challenging experiences that you're deeply interested in.

Here are a few life-changing projects to try instead of college:

- **Travel the world.** Traveling will give you an entirely new perspective, and exposure to new cultures always gives you something interesting to talk about with other people. Visit places you've only read about, eat food you don't recognize, and make friends with people you otherwise wouldn't have met. It's good for you.

- **Start a business.** The number one thing that starting a business will teach you is that failure is inevitable, and once you can get over that, you'll have a much better chance at succeeding the next time. This is old-school character building. Starting a business is also a great way to learn how to negotiate when people don't like you, and how to convince other people to help you. What you'll learn in this book will be immensely helpful if this is the route you choose.

- **Volunteer extensively.** Find a cause that you really care about and give back in the biggest way possible. Help build houses in your community. Tutor kids after school. But don't just dabble; treat it like a job. Give everything you have. Be a good human for no reason. It feels great—and you also learn a lot about yourself and others.

- **Become fluent in a new language.** No, not in the half-hearted way you tackled high school Spanish. REALLY learn one. Work on becoming fluent, start to enjoy pieces of the culture that are typically reserved for native speakers (telenovelas, anyone?), and then take an extended vacation to a country where that language is spoken.

- **Create art.** Painting, music, dance, sculpture—find something that really speaks to you and do it every single day. Create something beautiful that you're proud of. Share it.

- **Compete in a sport.** Learn a martial art. Start bowling competitively or learn chess. Hell, start a running club in your neighborhood. Do something physical with your time and force yourself to get better and better. Track your progress. Compete in tournaments. This is also a great way to get in better shape without trying. I can personally vouch for bodybuilding and jiujitsu. They changed my life.

- **Become an expert at something that fascinates you.** Like quantum physics? Devote an entire year to learning everything you can about string theory and become well versed in space-time. Create your own research studies and get them published in a journal. "Regular" people don't do this. Be exceptional. Push your own intellectual boundaries and try to learn difficult concepts that scare you.
- **Write a book.** There's a good chance you won't know what the hell you were talking about when you read your work again in twenty years, but the main benefits of writing are meditation, reflection, and habit building. You learn to control your thoughts and dedicate a set amount of time to something every day.

All of these things can lead to an amazingly fulfilling career later down the road, no degree required. And you'll end up spending the same amount of time doing them, but rather than getting a piece of paper and a pat on the back, you'll develop a useful skill that you can create something with immediately. In the transactional world that we live in, being able to produce has never been more valuable. People care about what you can deliver, not what a piece of parchment says that you learned.

If you're reading this, there's a good chance you've probably already finished college. Or are in college right now. That's OK too. You don't have to drop out of school tomorrow or tear up your diploma in a fit of rage. It'd be funny to watch, but seriously, you don't have to.

It's also important to note that there are a few professions where a university degree is definitely required. For instance, I prefer that my physician would have a college education before he operates on my spleen. I'd prefer that an engineer would be rigorously tested before he builds the bridges I'm going to drive over. Heavily institutionalized fields like law, medicine, and engineering will probably always require some sort of professional training at the university level.

However, this DOES NOT mean that students in these fields should neglect intentional, self-directed personal development in areas like those I listed above. If anything, rigorous study in a professional field like medicine or law should enhance the urge to develop other areas of your life outside of school, since you now have powerful tools to help yourself and others with your work.

Whichever route you choose, you MUST start the process of rethinking what it means to do your "life's work"—a term too few of us use to describe our journey these days. What do you want the impact of your life to be? What type of uniquely meaningful work can you contribute to the world to leave it a little better than when you found it?

Figuring out the answers to these questions is your first step toward becoming a Rich20Something.

Quick Recap

Yes, it's easy to go to a job you don't like and occasionally notice a "glitch" in the system without actually doing anything about it. But successful people notice these glitches and take action to change themselves. That's usually the only remarkable thing about successful people we so often admire: They didn't wait to take massive action. It's pointless to hate them, because you're hating something, someone, that you could become if only you would step out of your comfort zone.

In the past, college was the "secure" path to a happy life. Go to college, get a job, stay in that job for forty years, get a pension, retire. But the game has changed, and now you can make your own rules. There are so many other things you can do: start a business, travel the world, learn a martial art, learn to speak a language fluently—take your pick. And there's a good chance that if you take your time, you can find something that you truly love, not just fall into a career that you sort of like. All for less than the cost of college. And who knows? Maybe instead of wasting time and money, you'll actually find something you really want to do. Every day. Your life's work. Isn't that worth it?

Notes from the Field

Matt Wilson, Cofounder and Chief Adventurer at Under30Experiences

When I tell people how I met Matt Wilson years ago, the running joke is that he and his business partner, Jared, started the company I always wanted to start: Under-30CEO, which is a website dedicated to young entrepreneurs. At the time, it was everything I wanted Rich20 to be . . . and THEN some.

Matt, Jared, and I became fast friends, and over the next few years we made a lot of really great content together. Eventually, they decided to branch out and do something totally different. They started a travel company called Under30Experiences, and in a crazy turn of events, Rich20Something ended up acquiring Under-30CEO.

Now Matt spends his time helping other people travel the world. I've been all over the world with U30X, and I'll be on another trip soon. Come meet me :)

You can check out where they'll be next at www.Under 30Experiences.com.

I've always wanted to build something larger than myself, and I wanted to create freedom for myself—freedom to live wherever I wanted, to do whatever I wanted, and to do it with whomever I wanted. But at some point I realized that this can be selfish, and unfulfilling, if what you do isn't actually helping anybody.

I didn't see the hard work I put in as some sort of sacrifice. And what about all the people that were partying while I was working—what were they sacrificing? A chance to create a life of freedom? I live in Costa Rica, away from my family, so some people might call that a sacrifice. But I don't. I created my business so I could do just this.

Over the last five years, through yoga and meditation, I've worked hard to quiet any mental chatter that says anything like I'm not good enough. This has been crucial in my success, because it allows me to let go of any kind of limiting belief. Lots of my previous limiting beliefs weren't me; they were from society, parents, teachers, friends, and even television. Observing my mind through yoga and meditation has helped me to rewire my brain to the point that I honestly believe I can do anything I set my mind to.

If you make it a philosophy of your business to test things and learn from the outcomes, there's no such thing as failure. There's only feedback. Our travel business started by posting a Facebook status seeing if people wanted to go to Iceland. People responded favorably, and we started accepting payments. That's how a business starts. And today, it's easier than ever to test ideas with little to no money, and almost little to no time.

One thing about me that's massively contributed to my success is my almost maniacal desire to make plans and stick to them. Whether it's going running in the pouring rain, learning to meditate, or moving to Costa Rica, learning Spanish, and taking surfing lessons, I do what I say I'm going to do, because I value integrity.

There's no such thing as an overnight success. We published over four thousand articles on Under30CEO .com. That's an enormous amount of content—and that's an understatement. Working that hard has taught me so much, but I'm glad I didn't realize how truly hard it would be. Maybe I wouldn't have even started.

I don't think everyone can or should be an entrepreneur, just like I don't think everyone could be an artist or a pastry chef or a writer. Do I think that everyone can and should understand owning and running a business, and build something for themselves? Yes. Absolutely. Because the world has changed. Self-employment, working from anywhere, and developing your online skills—whether that's social media or web design or any other online skill—are going to be crucial to a lot of people's success. And thanks to the Internet, all the information that you'll ever need to be successful in this way is available right now.

3

Money Is Easy

(NEW TRUTH #3)

If you don't find a way to make money
while you sleep, you will work until you die.
—*Warren Buffett*

KEY TAKEAWAYS:

$ If you think starting a business nowadays is difficult, be grateful you weren't born in the 1800s! Back then, you needed hundreds of thousands of dollars to get a business off the ground. Now, you can just use the Internet. It's invisible, it's free, and it has all of the knowledge that humans have ever compiled.

$ We've been conditioned to believe that it's hard to make money. But information on how to make it is everywhere now. What's actually hard is the execution of those ideas.

$ A million dollars a year is about $2,700 dollars a day. Not a crazy amount.

ONE OF THE BENEFITS of being born to a teenage mother is that everybody else in your family is also much younger in comparison to other families. My relatives are at least fifteen years younger than they should be.

I'm twenty-eight, and my mom is in her forties. I have an aunt who is only two years older than me. My great-grandparents, both in their nineties, are still alive as I'm writing this (and extremely talkative, by the way). When I was born, my great-great-grandmother was still kickin', and I got to meet her. Agnes Zobel, born in 1899. Can you imagine that?

Actually, 1899 wasn't that long ago—just a few generations back, even if you live in a young family like mine.

Have you ever met anybody born in the 1800s? If you're reading this right now, I doubt it! And until a few years ago, I'd never really considered meeting her a big deal. But it is. The more I think about it, the more I realize how far society has come in only a few short generations. It's mind-blowing.

What was it like to start a business during the late 1800s? In a word, brutal.

Yes, there were still hustlers getting ahead. But the grind was MUCH different back then. The sheer amount of effort you needed to exert, capital you needed to raise, and time you needed to invest to make anything significant happen was staggering.

And most importantly, you had to be absolutely RUTHLESS to get results. Even the era's greatest entrepreneurs were often at the mercy of the savage capitalistic climate and had limited, slow economic reach. *Entrepreneurship just a hundred years ago was literally feast or famine.*

There was no such thing as a "lifestyle" business. Work from the beach? John D. Rockefeller would laugh in your face! Make your own hours? Andrew Carnegie might slap you! It was kill or be killed.

The competition was stiff primarily because resources were finite. Nearly every business of that era depended on limited, expensive (often nonrenewable) natural resources and a massive amount of almost–slave labor to get off the ground. Coal, oil, steel, and manpower. There was only so much of each to go around—and you had to pry them from the grips of other money-hungry savages to get your share.

Monopolies were the name of the game, and many of the federal antitrust laws in the United States were created as a direct response to the titans of this age. When the US government finally broke up Rockefeller's gargantuan Standard Oil Company in 1911, it had to be divided into THIRTY-FOUR individual companies—including what are now Exxon, Chevron, Mobil, and Conoco. WTF?

You. Could. Not. Get. In.

If you wanted to start a railroad company, there were only so many locations to place your tracks—and there was a 100 percent chance that Cornelius Vanderbilt or some other magnate already controlled that space. To earn your spot at the table, you had to be willing to outmaneuver, outsmart, legally destroy, outright cheat, and, in some cases, physically fight the men you were competing against.

And I do mean men. It goes without saying: For women, minorities, or other disenfranchised people, starting a business was utterly out of the question.

Forget about "following your passion." Oh, you like writing? That's cute! Unless you're Charles Dickens, forget about making a living with the pen. Although his time was just before the 1800s, Benjamin Franklin had to set up his own freaking printing house with gigantic presses just to make pamphlets and distribute them locally in Philadelphia! How many of us would even know where to begin with an enterprise like that?

Bottom line: It was MUCH harder just a short time ago, and you needed hundreds of thousands of dollars (sometimes millions) just to get your idea off the ground. All this was only a FEW generations ago, back when my great-great-grandmother Agnes was a kid! This part of history was literally within arm's reach of me!

Now, compare that to 2017 (or whenever you're reading this book in the future). You wake up and open your laptop or pull out your smartphone, devices so affordable that almost everyone owns one or has access to one. You hop on the Internet, an "invisible" service that connects you to everybody in the world and that can instantaneously deliver the sum of all human knowledge to you while you're sitting on the toilet in the morning taking a crap. You can also watch hilarious videos of cats getting stuck in various awkward positions, ad infinitum.

From there, you can literally do anything you want—at virtually no risk. You can start your own blog, magazine, or television show using publicly available (read: free) software. You can buy, sell, and trade goods instantly with anybody in the world. You can seek the advice and counsel of your idols. You can find people who need what you provide and sell your services. Hell, you don't even have to make something physical anymore; you can package up your knowledge and sell that! All without leaving your home. And you can get paid the same day.

What's more, there is literally no real competition anymore: no need to punch someone's lights out to get a coal mine, no need for hostile takeovers or slave labor. You can play your own game, completely undisturbed, and win. Sure, there are other people out there who are doing what you want to do. But that's actually a good thing. If other people in your space are doing well, that simply means there are customers who want to buy what you're selling.

Thanks to the good old Internet, you can reach those customers and millions more just like them with a small or non-existent budget. Despite what the evening news tells you, there still is a very prominent middle class. And they'll be the ones buying your stuff.

Welcome to the unlimited, ever-expanding marketplace!

If the Carnegies, Rockefellers, and Vanderbilts of the world were alive today, they would be ALL OVER these opportunities. *But they aren't alive—you are.* Now it's your turn to take advantage. This is your unique opportunity in history to take control of your destiny.

That's why, of the Three New Truths, I believe the final truth to be the most powerful: *Money is easy.*

Money Is Easy; Executing Your Ideas Is Another Story . . .

The TV shows we watch, the songs we sing, and the clothes we wear are all designed to make us associate prestige and importance with money, so it follows that we'd also create the cultural myth that money is hard to acquire.

We have been conditioned to believe that making a lot of money is difficult. But it turns out nothing could be further from the truth. Let me ask you this: With so much information available about starting a business, and so many free resources for creating stunning content, marketing yourself, and finding new customers, how could it be that most people are still struggling to make more money?

The answer is simple: Execution of your ideas and the ability to follow through are the real keys to successfully earning more. The information alone is not enough. It's easy to make money, and every single tool and idea you need to start doing it right now is available for you to use—in many cases, for free. Yet none of that matters without execution.

Yes, it's true that compared to the 1800s, it is exponentially easier to get started now. And I made that point both to entertain you and to give you some perspective on how big your opportunity is. But even with that knowledge, you still have to act. You still have to get off the couch. That is the key to all of this. That is the key to this entire book.

If you've ever been upset because you feel like you're not getting paid what you deserve, or you want to start a side hustle, or you don't know how to get started on your business idea, just know that the biggest skills at your disposal will be hunger and perseverance.

The money is easy. It will come. I promise. *My question to you is, can you manage your time and execute a plan?* Can you quickly and efficiently sketch out what you'd like to do with your time, prioritize what needs to be done, and start researching all the things you don't know?

Next, can you then learn when it's time to stop researching and start acting? Can you continue with the plan for as long as necessary, and make necessary adjustments in the face of repeated rejections? Can you stand strong when the universe is testing you and rise to challenges instead of slinking away from them?

If you can do all that, you have what it takes. If not, you'll always be left wondering why your ideas never pan out. *Money is easy. Once you have perseverance and execution down to a science, the money will follow as a natural side effect of your relentless hustle.*

One Million Dollars, the Easy Way

Some goals seem freaking impossible until we sit down and literally break down how they can be accomplished. You have to take apart each component, understand it, and then reverse engineer it into your life.

Making money is no different. Barring some outliers, you don't just "become" a millionaire. No millionaire fairy godmother is going to just drop the money into your bank account. Can you imagine that? *"Oh, hey . . . here's your million. Sorry for the delay. I've been busy all morning dropping off everyone else's million-dollar checks!"*

It's a gradual process. It starts with a good idea. That idea doesn't have to be something original; it just has to be something that other people actually want or need . . . *and something that you like enough to do every day without stopping.*

Then you start doing that thing every day. You find a way to help other people with that thing. You help them so much that they tell their friends. And their friends' friends. You start making some money, and then a little more, and then a little more every day—until one day you look and a little has become a lot.

And when you look at all the people you've helped, you realize that number is a lot too. That's the secret: *You have to help a lot of people to make a lot of money.*

To make a million dollars, you have to help so many people that your work generates about $2,700 every day for 365 days straight. That number might seem hilariously impossible to you right now, but think again.

Let's do the math: If every person you helped gave you one dollar, you'd need to help approximately 2,700 people every day to make a million dollars a year. If everyone you helped gave you two dollars, now you'd only need to help about 1,400 people per day. Imagine if each person gave you five dollars, or ten! Suddenly it becomes a bit easier. Are you starting to see the pattern here? It's not the making money part that's hard. It's the consistency over time. It's the follow-through.

So here's the deal: You want to be a millionaire? Fine! You'll need $2,740 today, tomorrow, and the 363 days after that. It's just math. Now, it's time to find a few thousand people who need your help. Are you up to the task?

Anything you want in the world can be yours, if only you'd break it down into tiny little chunks.

Quick Recap

You should thank your lucky stars that you're reading this book today. Just a few generations ago, most of the things you're capable of or allowed to do now would have been damn near impossible. To start a business in the 1800s, you had to be utterly ruthless, prepare for brutal competition, and have lots of money and/or resources. It was insanely difficult.

If you were a woman or a minority? Forget about it. Wasn't going to happen. But now? Now we have the Internet, which is essentially infinite, and has all the knowledge you could ever need. See, it's not hard to make money. That's a myth. Money is easy. The hard part is execution. Can you design a plan and stick to it? If you can, money will be a natural by-product of your hustle.

Notes from the Field

Joshua Jordison, Founder of the Circle

As you read about more of my experiences throughout this book, you'll see that much of the "luck" that I stumbled upon is the direct result of people I've met along the way—and more specifically, how I've been able to deliver immense value in order to make friends in "high places."

Nobody wields this skill with more precision and genuine care than my friend JJ.

Joshua is a master connector, and he really understands what makes people tick, because although he started from the bottom, he spent much of his life learning how to make powerful friends.

His story is one we can all learn from.

Check out what he's up to at www.JoshuaJordison.com and www.jointhecircle.co.

When I was seven years old, I woke up in the middle of the night to commotion downstairs. I walked into the living room and saw my dad on the floor, covered in blood. He'd been shot. My neighbors, who were meth dealers, thought my dad had called the police on them, even though he hadn't. My dad had been volunteering at a center for underprivileged youth, and as he was walking to his car to come home, some men with guns approached him. They told him to get out of the car. My dad didn't. He tried to drive away as quickly as possible, and they shot at him. A bullet hit him in the arm. It wasn't fatal, and the ambulance eventually came and took him to the hospital, where they patched him up, but seeing that as a seven-year-old had an impact on me.

It had an impact on me because even though this happened, my family and I were still stuck. And we were stuck because we couldn't afford to move anywhere safer.

So . . . that's my why. That's always been my why. My family's safety.

Now, at twenty-nine years old, I've been able to help my parents buy a house in Orange County. A house worth north of one million dollars. And they're safe.

The most important thing I've had to sacrifice is stability, which hasn't been easy, given what I've just told you about how unstable my childhood was. I could've worked in corporate America and made good money—I had plenty of opportunities to do so—but I didn't want to sell my life and soul to a corporation.

So, if I had to, I would absolutely do it all again. Actually, as I look back on my twenties, my only regret is not taking more risks. Every goal I set—even the ones I thought would be impossible—I've achieved. So I'm learning how to set even bigger goals.

In my early twenties, I would've said the first things you should do when starting a business are incorporate your company, raise money, all that kind of stuff. Now? Find out who your customers are, and get one of them to buy from you. Because it's important to first find out if you actually have something that's valuable to people. And now you can do that without putting any real resources into it; you just need to spend your time doing research.

To be in business, you need to be able to sell. You need to be able to connect with people and get them to buy what you have. Another way to think of being a salesperson: If you have something that people want, and you're not telling them about it, you're doing them a disservice.

One of the most difficult parts of my entrepreneurial journey was what my parents thought about it at the beginning. They were angry, and they didn't understand why I was dropping out of college to be an "entrepreneur."

And that lasted for a few years. It's hard when the people who love you don't understand you.

Maybe related to that, the biggest excuse that I had to overcome is that I'm not good enough. That I somehow don't deserve this life I've created. That what I have to say isn't worth listening to. Logically, I know it's not true. But emotionally, it's still there. I'm 95 percent past this, and I'm working on that last 5 percent.

Something about who I am that's helped me be successful is my ability to handle risk, and stress, and being able to manage my emotions. I developed it at a young age out of necessity. And now, the worst day I have as an entrepreneur is better than the best day I had while I was a child. There are very few things related to being an entrepreneur that I wouldn't be able to handle.

Being successful, to me, means being free from worry. It means being safe. It means having enough money to help yourself and the people you love. It started off as just being the amount of money I could make, but as I got a bit older, I started understanding that you can be free from things that money will never be able to free you from—worrying, for example. If you have lots of money but don't have the ability to control your emotions, I don't think that's success.

4

Focus and Get Going: How to Eliminate Distraction and Crush Your Goals

People think focus means saying yes to the thing you've got to focus on. But that's not what it means at all. It means saying no to the hundred other good ideas that there are. You have to pick carefully. —Steve Jobs

KEY TAKEAWAYS:

$ We're forgetting to develop the ability to focus intensely and complete one single task from beginning to end.

$ There are so many different ways to get in touch with people, RIGHT NOW, that we're forgetting that we also have the choice not to interact, and instead to focus.

$ Lions, one of the earth's greatest hunters, spend twenty hours a day sleeping, lounging, or having sex. That leaves four hours for hunting, otherwise known as "work."

$ Stop thinking of "hustle" and start thinking of "calculated hustle," because success isn't about relentless hard work for an indefinite period of time; it's about knowing when and how to be relentless in working hard, and knowing when and how to recharge with downtime.

$ Learn to ride the "motivation wave" and learn the art of ruthless prioritization.

FOR TWENTY YEARS, filmmaker Sooyong Park has devoted his life to the study, recording, and preservation of the wild Siberian tiger. Two to three times a year, he leaves his family for months at a time to stay in the frozen forests of eastern Russia, Manchuria, and the Korean Peninsula, in hopes of catching a glimpse of the great cats.

To withstand temperatures of −30°C, he builds himself an underground igloo, reinforced with sticks. To sustain himself, he packs hundreds of tiny rations of nuts and seeds in plastic wrap. When he's thirsty, he drinks the snow. (In case you're wondering, inside the igloo there's a small "toilet" area to pee and poop.)

Then he takes out his camera and waits. Sometimes days, sometimes weeks, sometimes months—waiting for the goddamn tigers to show up. But even when they do show up, he's not allowed to show his excitement. He has to be absolutely focused in hopes of getting one fleeting picture without scaring them away (or getting himself killed).

And Sooyong's unconventional ability to focus on his work with tigers has gotten the world some of the rarest footage ever captured of tiger behavior in the wild. Among his best finds, Park has captured pictures of tigers giving birth in the wild, playing with each other at various ages, and doing other incredible things that nobody in the world had been able to record before.

After watching a documentary about him, I immediately started thinking about what it must be like to focus on one thing so intensely for such a long period of time. It blew my mind!

Imagine being alone in that igloo twenty-four hours a day, seven days a week. No updates on social, no contact, no toilet. *"Day forty-seven, still waiting on tigers. Anyone else up? Lol!"*

The funny thing is, it's a GOOD thing he was so isolated out there.

Having contact with the outside world and constantly being wrapped up in the flow of daily gossip sound bites would have robbed him of the chance to actually focus on what he came to see. And the same thing is happening to you and me every single day.

Focusing in today's world is harder than ever.

Unlike Sooyong Park, most of us have jobs that don't require us to be out in nature for extended periods of time, which makes it much harder to escape the social media tractor beam. Most people can't even complete a single task from beginning to end. It's no surprise, really. Just take a look at your environment. The way that our culture and society are set up is not conducive to maintaining discipline or focus, partly because we've made ourselves increasingly available to outside intrusion.

A few decades ago, there were just a handful of ways to contact each other: snail mail, home telephone, or in person.

That was it. Fast-forward to today, and there are infinite ways to check in on somebody that you want to talk to.

On my phone alone I have:

1. the Apple iMessage app (for personal texts)
2. Facebook Messenger (for Facebook direct messages)
3. a Facebook app (for comments and updates)
4. a Twitter app
5. Facebook Mentions (for fan page messages and updates)
6. WhatsApp (for international texts and calls)
7. Snapchat (for nudes?)
8. Instagram (for more direct messages)
9. Skype (for group calls and international video chat)
10. GroupMe (I use it for social media interest groups)
11. Kik (strictly for communicating with Instagram partners)
12. Gmail (email)

That's twelve different ways to get in touch with me at any given moment—not including making an actual phone call! That, my friends, is DESIGNED distraction.

Everything in our lives is brilliantly designed to keep us coming back for more—while getting less and less done. It's almost impossible to avoid. This isn't an excuse to fall into Candy Crush oblivion and never return; it's just a fact. *The technology you use every single day is designed to drain your focus and decrease your attention span.*

Teams of people engineer the technology that you use at home, at work, and on the go, and their ONLY job is to figure out how to make you click, share, swipe, watch, consume, and ultimately make them money. It's a tough, if not impossible, battle to win.

But here's the good news: We are now in the idea generation. Ideas have become the commodity of choice.

Ideas are free to produce. And good ideas, followed by focused execution, are the basis for our entire economy now. In fact, if you can keep your attention trained on one idea for an extended period of time—especially when it's high-level work—you can surpass 99 percent of your peers and people in your field.

With so much distraction, uninterrupted focus is a rare superpower these days.

One of my friends, Daniel Thomas Hind, says it this way: "Give the greatest philosophers of ancient history Facebook and I'll show you all the books they didn't write."

Developing Focus by Creating

Focus is learned skill and attention plus mental dexterity. It can be developed like a muscle, and the more you consistently train this skill, the easier it becomes to "switch on."

The most common response to lack of focus is attempting to use your will to overpower the distraction. Maybe you even delete annoying apps and pledge to check your messages only every fortnight. These ideas sound good, but we know they never end up working long-term.

Eventually, you'll have to use your apps. And you're going to want to check your email. Being focused isn't about cultivating greater willpower or hoping that the world goes back to a "simpler" time.

You're most likely going to be on social media. This is just part of our new social ecosystem. Get over it. Most of us want to use these tools, so it's not about eliminating them; it's about learning how to adapt our lives to them. What you spend your time on is a result of what you do habitually. If you can change your habits, you can increase your ability to focus and change your entire life.

I've found that the following two principles have helped me dramatically increase my focus and prioritize what's important in my life.

Principle 1: Learn to Ride the "Motivation Wave" for as Long as Possible

Stanford professor B. J. Fogg looks at motivation a bit differently than most. In Fogg's model, motivation is a wave with peaks and valleys, and the goal isn't to stay at a constant peak but rather to recognize the valleys and adjust your effort accordingly.

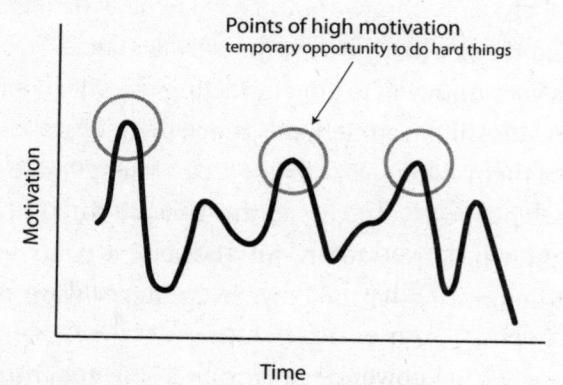

Fogg's Motivational Wave Model

According to Fogg, it's not realistic to expect focused attention from yourself at all times. Instead, the key is to become more aware of your daily (or even hourly) fluctuations in motivation, and do the hardest things in your day when you're feeling the best.

For example, you might use this approach to "trick" yourself into working out every morning. You know that when you get up in the morning and you've just had your first meal, your willpower is at the highest point it will be all day. You haven't checked your email yet or jumped into the shitstorm that is social media. If you hurry up and get to the gym, you can take full advantage of the natural motivation wave that hits you first thing in the morning, and if you ride it carefully, you can surf those feelings of optimism and maintain your energy until twelve or one o'clock in the afternoon.

In anticipation of this wave, you'll stack all your hardest work between ten and one o'clock. All the calls you don't want to make, all the tedious emails you don't want to answer, and all the boring work you have to plow through—you need to do them when you're at your peak state.

If you wait until you're already feeling the afternoon dip to start force-feeding yourself the most dreaded tasks, you'll never get them done. Do what you can when you're feeling good; then purposely find easier things to do when your wave is dying down. If you zoom out and look at your life on a month-to-month basis, you'll see even bigger wave patterns over time.

In fact, you'll probably notice that just a handful of key events create most of the progress you'll make all year:

- You get a promotion at work.
- You lose your first fifteen pounds.
- You have your first "100 visitors" day on your website.

These are like mini growth spurts that serve as the high point of your motivation wave.

Pay careful attention so that you know when you're in one of these growth spurts. Ride high on that motivation wave and use focused intensity to get as much done as you can while you're feeling good.

Later, when the inevitable dip comes, you'll be able to coast off the progress you made the month before. Once you've learned to anticipate these frequent ups and downs, you'll know how to take advantage of them and you won't be a slave to the motivational roller coaster.

Principle 2: Learn the Art of Ruthless Prioritization

One of the biggest struggles millennials face is wading through the information overload to figure out what we should be doing with our time—and can you really blame us?

Every time you look at your phone, dozens of pings, notifications, and alerts flood the screen. All of them seem urgent. All of them could be important. So we spend entire days, weeks, and months approaching these conflicting demands without any specific prioritization.

Like a grocery list, we throw items into our basket, check them off the list, and hope we didn't forget anything. But if you want to truly hone your focus, you'll need a new approach that champions specificity and ruthless prioritization. The goal is to cut through all the distractions and work only on the core items that will actually move your life forward.

How to determine what you should spend your time on

If you take nothing else from this chapter, remember this: Your life is not a grocery list. You shouldn't just seek to check off your to-do's and call it a day.

Your day is not a collection of random tasks. Not everything on your plate holds equal importance, and that means many seemingly urgent items may need to fall by the wayside while you work on the small number of objectives that really matter. *Once you really understand this concept at a core level, life gets a LOT simpler.*

More often than not, beginning entrepreneurs confuse "motion" with progress and work on things that don't move the needle. They do things to make themselves feel productive and accomplished.

For example:

- **Opening a business checking account the first week—** with no money to put into it. But it's nice to have that debit card. It feels official, right?
- **Starting Twitter and Facebook accounts.** Gotta have a "presence" on social media. Bonus points if you go on some shady website and buy three thousand robot fans from India.
- **Agonizing for weeks or even months over domain**

names, brand names, or logos—because you read an article in *Fast Company* about the importance of branding.

■ **Ordering two thousand business cards**—with the logo that you agonized over. Then, after you pass out twelve, you realize that you actually hate them. The cards sit on the top shelf of your closet until you move.

■ **Creating an LLC, S corp, etc.**—you know, for tax purposes.

None of these make a damn bit of difference in the beginning. And trust me, I'm laughing as I write this because I've done ALL of them. It took me years to realize that I was really doing them to inflate my own ego and sense of accomplishment, all the while actually avoiding meaningful work.

So what types of things deserve your time and attention?

If you're starting a business, your main focus should be anything that makes money or leads directly to making money. That's it.

This might include things like:

■ Setting up meetings with potential customers
■ Making cold calls, knocking on doors, or sending inquiries via email
■ Working your referral network of friends, family, and colleagues to find people who need your products or services
■ Creating content designed to attract your ideal customers
■ Doing client work

These are the HARD things. They are uncomfortable. They're not flashy. But they make money. And you don't need to do them a million times to start seeing results. There will be tons of other things that pop up in your day. Emails will flood in, distractions will arise, and other objectives will creep onto your list of priorities. That's fine—add those things to the list. But never forget that you have only a limited amount of time each day to get things done. *Focus on things that result in you getting paid.*

For instance, yesterday I did a brain dump into my notebook, and these were the objectives I came up with for the day:

1. Follow up with editors (for five different online publications)
2. Client meeting
3. Add widget back to the website
4. Return emails
5. Write two thousand words for a megapost
6. Upload new videos to my Freelance Domination course
7. Write Wednesday–Friday posts for the blog

It's tempting to write this list down and immediately start hacking away at it linearly like a shopping list. But that's not the smartest way.

If I look at it, I can see that some items are moneymakers, so they need to come first. Others take more mental energy; they need to happen at the beginning of the day, while I'm fresh. Some are just things that I want to do, but that won't really move me forward per se.

Let's say I redid the list based on what's actually important.

The new list would look like this:

1. Client meeting
2. Upload new videos to my Freelance Domination course
3. Write Wednesday–Friday posts for the blog
4. Write two thousand words for a megapost
5. Follow up with editors (for five different online publications)
6. Return emails
7. Add widget back to the website

Notice that the three things directly related to making income are now prioritized first, followed by the most intellectually challenging items, followed by the more rote tasks.

Now, this list is set up so that even if I finish only HALF of the items, the most important things are taken care of. This is the level of prioritization that you should design your days with, so that even during an "off" day you're still making progress. Once you've learned how to think about your day and determine which things are truly important, it's time to make your list of priorities even smaller.

Getting Ruthless with Your Priorities by Shrinking Your List

Remember this: *Simple to-do lists are powerful. Long to-do lists are DISEMPOWERING.*

Once you've prioritized your list according to what actually moves the needle, I want you to cut that list in half.

The reasons for this are both pragmatic and psychological. Using the previous to-do list, think about what's going on in the background. If I start with this list, and I am only able to work through about half (which is pretty typical any given day), it looks like this:

1. ~~Client meeting~~
2. ~~Upload new videos to my Freelance Domination course~~
3. ~~Write Wednesday–Friday posts for the blog~~
4. Write two thousand words for a megapost
5. Follow up with editors (for five different online publications)
6. Return emails
7. Add widget back to the website

I got some major things done. That's solid work! But looking at this list in its current state, I feel bad about my own progress. Why? Because I've done less than half of what I intended to accomplish for the day. Psychologically, this is defeating to see, not to mention unmotivating.

If I make long lists like this day after day and never finish, I'll always feel like I'm behind. I'll always feel unaccomplished. But what would happen if we chopped this list in half?

I feel SO much better about this list:

1. ~~Client meeting~~
2. ~~Upload new videos to my Freelance Domination course~~
3. ~~Write Wednesday–Friday posts for the blog~~

This is a fully completed to-do list. This is a successful day. This is something I can build on. And if I get to any of items 4–7, it feels like a BONUS. **You can actually get more done by getting less done.** What a change in perspective! (Note: One of my favorite authors, Charles Duhigg, advocates a similar type of process for getting more done by doing less in his book *Smarter Faster Better*.)

Think about it this way: Whether you accomplish three out of seven things in your day, or three out of three, you're still completing the SAME amount of work. You're getting the most important things done, the things that will make the biggest impact on your career, your success, and your happiness. But one list leaves you feeling empty and dissatisfied, while the other leaves you confident and happy with your daily progress. So which list will you choose?

Quick Recap

Cultivating the ability to focus intentionally on a single task, from beginning to end, is becoming a lost art, and perhaps even a lost superpower in today's world. One reason we've lost it is because we have so many apps that let us talk to all of our friends right this second. And we seem to have forgotten that we also have the choice to put our phones down, not talk to them, and actually give all our focus to doing one thing.

We must learn how to ride the motivation wave through the inevitable ups and downs, and then learn to say no to things that don't move us forward— especially in our business. That's the only way to do your best work.

Notes from the Field

Maneesh Sethi, Founder and CEO of Pavlok

There's no better person to wrap up a chapter on intentional focus than my friend Maneesh. A few years ago, he hit me up on Gchat (when that was a thing) with a crazy idea. He wanted to create a wearable device that would train you to adopt better habits—with electric shocks.

Everyone thought he was crazy. Yet just a few short years later, Pavlok is a legitimate player in the wearable technology space, has made millions in revenue, has been featured in every conceivable media outlet in the world, and—most importantly—actually helps people break bad habits! I was proud to be a part of the early Pavlok team—so much so, in fact, that I got a Pavlok tattoo. It's kinda crazy. Next time you see me, ask to see it.

You can learn more about Pavlok at www.Pavlok.com.

I think people's "why" changes throughout their life. First, for me, it was about what new, shiny object I could get, or how could I get more money. Then it became about freedom, mainly in the form of traveling. And now it's about helping people to change their behavior. I've never been able to get control over my own habits, so I want to help other people get control over theirs.

I would 100 percent do it all again if I had to, because it's the biggest and most challenging thing I can do for the world. And it's just "me."

I suppose I knew I was an entrepreneur because I've always wanted to make money. When I was in middle school, I was buying video games from people and selling them online for a profit. Also, I was never able to do anyone else's work for them, and I got fired a lot.

The most difficult part of my journey has been getting myself to do the stuff I know I should be doing. It seems like the more important something is, the more I have to convince myself to do it. But I suppose that's why Pavlok was invented in the first place.

I've been close to giving up a few times, mostly when we've been down to a month's or even a week's worth of cash. But every time I managed to figure out a solution. One time I even sold some alpha prototypes just to keep Pavlok in business. I didn't give up, because I genuinely thought Pavlok was the best idea I'd ever had. And anyway, I'd started to hire people. So I had to persist—because I had to pay them.

Being successful is doing what's awesome to you. If you're a nurse, maybe your "awesome" is taking care of your patients so they're still able to feel happy. If you're a father, maybe your "awesome" is taking care of your kid with all your love. My own "awesome" used to be traveling around the world and being the coolest guy in the room. Now, it's more about building a product that people get incredible value from.

The most important thing entrepreneurs can do is value their time. If you want to be a million-dollar CEO, then value your time like a million-dollar CEO would. How much value is that half-hour meeting really going to bring you? Would a million-dollar CEO attend it?

Something about who I am that's contributed to my success is that I'm a very distracted person. It means I can learn things rapidly, and that I also have an inability to finish things. That's probably why Pavlok is a product where hardware meets software meets psychology meets fitness meets personality types.

I wouldn't say anything to myself on the day I first started my business, because it would only make me fuck up everything.

5

How to Give Up Fear and Prepare for Your Journey

I think the one skill people need that they don't know they need is the ability to manage their emotions. There are so many things you have to deal with as an entrepreneur that you just never have to deal with as an employee, and so your responsibility increases enormously. That's why you need to be able to handle the ups and downs.
—*Srini Rao*
 Founder, Unmistakable Creative
 https://unmistakablecreative.com

KEY TAKEAWAYS

$ Being uncomfortable doesn't mean you're going to die, and it doesn't mean that you have to let fear make your decisions for you.

$ We need to give fear less power in our lives.

$ The resistance you feel isn't a red light. It's a green one. And that means it's time to GO!

$ Be ready to take advantage of "inflection points." If

you do, your business will never be the same, because you can't undo the massive leaps in progress you'll make.

$ Being inspired and motivated just isn't enough.

EVERY MORNING, I put my hands around another man's neck and try to choke him to death. It feels so good. I always look forward to it.

That's what's so great about jiujitsu: Since there is no striking (mostly just chokes, joint locks, etc.), you get to test your limits at full speed without worrying about getting brain damage on a regular basis. But I'll admit, the learning curve can be terrifying at first.

Apparently, lying on a mat with a two-hundred-pound human on top of you, slowly constricting your airflow, is not something that many people are used to experiencing. The feeling invokes an evolutionary, involuntary fear that for some people is overwhelming. Most people quit after a few classes.

But for freaks like me who end up sticking around for a while, something strange and wonderful begins to happen: You eventually chill the fuck out. *You begin to realize that even if you're uncomfortable, you're not going to die.* You develop a much better barometer for when you're actually out of oxygen and when an opponent is just "bothering your neck" (the masochistic term fellow jiujitsu players use for strangling an opponent).

You begin to relax, and the entire process starts to become fun. It turns into a game. You tap out, learn what you did wrong, and keep rolling. You eventually stop letting fear govern your decisions—and that's when you can finally start making the important choices that define how good you'll become at the sport.

Your approach toward changes in your life should be the same way.

Fear is the constant companion of successful people throughout history. Always has been, always will be. It's an indication of risk, and risk is the precursor to progress. Beware: If you use fear as an indicator for whether you should do something, if you change your mind every time you feel the prickly tingle of "afraid," you'll constantly withdraw from situations where you need to be giving yourself fully. You'll never be your best you.

I think we all need to give a lot less power to fear in our lives.

When to Make Your Move

Here's the reality: You will almost always be scared to make big changes in your life. But there's a huge difference between being afraid and simply being uncertain. It's OK to be uncertain.

In fact, if you're feeling uncertain about a decision, that can actually be a very powerful sign that you're on the right track. After all, an overabundance of certainty in your life will probably lead you to more of what you're already doing. That's called stagnation.

Case in point: quitting your job to work on your passion.

People often ask me if they should quit their jobs or, better yet, when they'll know it's the "right" time to cut bait and leave for the greener pastures of entrepreneurship. My response is always "maybe" and "it depends."

The ideal situation is that you quit your job with enough money to fall back on and with a solid plan that you've tested first and are ready to execute. In a perfect world, you'd start a side hustle, scale it up slowly, and then "turn up the knob" gradually until your part-time hustle income begins to rival your full-time income—maybe until it reaches 60 to 70 percent, where at the bare minimum you can cover your living expenses.

At that point, you'll know the only thing holding you back from taking your business full-time is your regular job. At that point, you can quit. If you can take this path, by all means DO IT. It will make the whole process much less stressful.

But this is real life. The transition is rarely that smooth. You will be faced with resistance to making the leap, and you must not let fear or other people's limitations hold you in place at the pivotal moment.

Sometimes you just have to go!

Do You Have the "Go! Factor"?

In 2003, the Human Genome Project was hailed a massive success. We'd officially mapped out the genetic makeup of human DNA with 99.9 percent accuracy.

It doesn't matter who you are, where you came from, or what your mother's maiden name is—scientists now know with astonishing certainty what you look like under a microscope. But does that mean we can grow another you in a petri dish? Hardly.

We're still toying with the complexities and complications of re-creating individual organs, let alone cloning an entire human being. It's strange, actually. We know all the ingredients that make up a person, down to the molecule. We also know the exact order and proportion those ingredients need to be arranged in. Yet even with all that knowledge, we can't figure out how to make a new human!

What's missing from our recipe? Life. I like to call this the "Go! factor."

When your genetic material is taking shape in the womb, things don't always fit together perfectly. Maybe there are even some conditions or inconveniences you were born with that you wish you could change. But your cells don't care about any of that.

Their only goal is to create life, then ship it to the world. Go!

There is no permission sought. Consequences be damned. Go!

There is no weighing of pros and cons or worrying about ifs and whens. Go!

"Defects" will be dealt with later. Or not at all. Go!

The only goal is to ship the project. The project of you. Since you're alive to read this right now, your body made the right decision. But sometimes your mind isn't as smart as your body. It's a shame that in our fully formed state, most of us can't harness such a painfully obvious approach as Go! to bring our own ideas to life.

The difference between ideas that become real, breathing

entities—ideas that become books, speeches, and businesses—and those that die in the mind is Go! And right now, our generation is low on Go! We're in dreadfully short supply, matter of fact.

Why? I think it's because we've mistaken filling up the car with gas for actually making the road trip. *We've confused the exhaustion we feel from planning to act with the exhaustion that comes from actually acting.*

We also build high walls to defend ourselves from our lack of Go! One way to build a wall is to insulate yourself with inspirational books, YouTube tutorials, and endless research so well that you actually forget that you haven't done anything. Try it. It works!

You can also try to protect yourself from lack of Go! by investing all your energy into studying those who have a lot of it. If you invest enough energy, you'll begin to feel like you're moving too. It's a wonderful vicarious experience, like licking the spoon when your mom is making cookies: You get just a taste of the real experience. It's not the real thing, though.

You laugh, cry, and shout for your favorite athletes when they score. You cheer for your favorite actors and celebrities at the theater and on television. You wait with bated breath for luminaries like Steve Jobs and Elon Musk to reveal the Next Big Thing.

Possibilities and grand visions stream into your brain, and you begin to feel energized. Oh shit, there's a possibility that you might actually Go! this time. Then, instead of taking that newfound energy and using it to create something of your own, you diffuse it by reaching for the remote.

Click. *Whew, that was close.* You've been waiting way too long to Go! It's time to stop sabotaging yourself. The tension you feel when transitioning from "at rest" to "in motion" isn't a warning sign that the machine is about to break; it's the necessary force you have to overcome to leave your own atmosphere. Get some thrust.

The concept of Go! is so simple that I'm getting frustrated just writing about it. You can apply Go! to anything, big or small. One common mistake is thinking that only big projects count. But you don't need to start a million-dollar business, drop a number one album, or win the Ironman to activate your Go! at full capacity.

Maybe the process for reporting your sales numbers at work is tedious and time-consuming. You know that a few formulas in a spreadsheet will save hours and dollars. Do it today. Like, now. Like, right now. Don't delay. Then show your team and ask them for feedback.

Every time you go to the gym, you pass the Zumba class and look through the window. It looks like they're having so much fun! You'd like to join, but you don't want to look like a fool. Wouldn't it be better to wait until you practiced at home a bit first? No. No, it wouldn't be better, actually. Turn around this instant, walk into that room, and join the class right now. (Stand in the back if you're nervous.)

By using your Go! power on smaller projects, you'll become increasingly comfortable with saying yes to yourself and breaking through the learned inertia and malaise of our culture.

Here's the real key: Choosing to Go! is choosing change, change for yourself and change for the world around you.

Change is scary and uncomfortable. Everyone knows this. Ask Martin. Ask Gandhi. Ask Elon. Ask Oprah. But the resistance you feel, the fear you feel, the uncertainty you feel—those aren't red lights telling you to stop what you're doing. Those are the green lights telling you that you're about to cross through the intersection of where you are and where you want to be.

Step on the gas. Go!

Steve Kamb on Getting Started Now

The first thing someone should do when starting a business is start. Today. Whatever you do, whether it's building a website or launching your blog or writing your book, it's probably going to be terrible. So you might as well launch sooner rather than later and get feedback and improve it.

Steve Kamb

Founder, Nerd Fitness

www.nerdfitness.com

Don't Let Other People's "Requirements" Psych You Out of Pursuing Your Dream

One of my old acting coaches in Tampa, Kathy Laughlin, maintained that all students must complete a special "Hollywood checklist" before moving out to Los Angeles and attempting to make it big.

I can't remember exactly what the list entailed, but it was something like:

- You need to have at least fifteen thousand dollars in the bank.
- You need x number of supporting roles in other films so that you have some credibility.
- You need an agent in LA before you move.
- You need to have mastered the basics of witchcraft and alchemy.

I'm only naming a few of the requirements; the list was pretty extensive.

I'll admit, the ideas here aren't horrible, and they were created as a guidepost to help students have the greatest chance of success when going to LA. It was an admirable effort on Kathy's part. Interestingly enough, though, I noticed that the checklist often had the opposite effect on people.

Instead of using the requirements on this list as a framework to get started, students took them as immutable law—and attached paralyzing fear to the outcome!

"Oh crap, I only have thirteen thousand dollars in savings! I'm not ready! I can't move out to California yet, because Kathy said so!"

"I need to wait until I get at least three more callbacks to even consider moving!"

How many of these students do you think ever made it out to LA? Not many.

The crazy thing is that even if you have all the elements in the checklist lined up, it certainly doesn't guarantee success at acting in LA—far from it, in fact. And on the flip side, many people have gone out to Hollywood without any checklists or credentials and somehow still made it.

Either way you look at the situation, it's a matter of chance and hustle. So why not bet on yourself to win? If your dream is to become a Hollywood movie star, then own that dream. Don't shrink away from your own ambitions because you couldn't check off a few boxes on an arbitrary list.

I wonder how many students would have made it but were too scared to take the leap because they hadn't checked off everything on that list. Better yet, I wonder how many people continue to operate their lives with fear as a guiding principle, or wait until everything is "perfect" to do their life's work?

Very rarely are you going to have all the elements perfectly aligned to make your move, and this will most likely cause you to be afraid of failure. In some cases, you might not even have all the information you need to make the best decision! But the universe favors the bold. It favors creation over stagnation. No matter how long you try to wait it out, it's still your turn. We're all playing this cosmic board game together, and you have to make a move. You must learn how to take calculated risks with speed and decisiveness.

And above all, you have to believe in yourself, even when others don't. Especially when others don't.

Recognizing and Leveraging Inflection Points

There are no real secrets in the success game, but there are what I call "inflection points." Once you get over your own fears and self-doubt, you'll be able to recognize them very clearly and capitalize on them. Let me explain.

One of the things that always perplexed me about business (especially the online world) was how it seemed like some people just EXPLODED onto the scene. They went from zero to one hundred really quick, everything they did online seemed to work, and, from an outside perspective, it seemed like they were riding a perpetual growth curve.

Consider my beginnings as a blogger. I was just writing away in my dark room, getting precisely zero readers every single day. Then a few of my pieces got traction. It wasn't because of any specific plan, to be honest. It was just the result of swinging the ax at the same tree over and over.

But there is a catch here: I had gotten enough practice to know what resonated with people.

Assuming you're doing the right things, like working on projects you care about, being meticulous about getting the word out, and constantly improving the quality of your work, you will create material that resonates with people. Then, eventually you will hit an inflection point.

It's kind of like puberty: spontaneous, unavoidable, usually uneven growth that can change everything literally overnight. The inflection point could come from an article, video, or podcast that goes viral. It could come from influencers who find your idea/product/service and tell their audiences. It could come because of a discovery you make that introduces something entirely new to the world.

It's often an accident, or the result of something you didn't think was a big deal at the time. But your inflection point WILL occur with enough time in the game. You WILL break through. It's just a rule of the universe. Everyone gets this opportunity.

When that happens, BE READY. RECOGNIZE the opportunity for what it is.

The inflection point is your opportunity to take control of your trajectory and make sure that your message gets out there. If you aren't prepared to have the attention of the whole world on you, then when you get it for fifteen minutes, you'll squander it! Don't risk losing the momentum. Pounce on it relentlessly.

There are two amazing things about inflection points. Number one: If you capitalize on them, your business (and your life) will never be the same. There is no undoing the kind of growth that being featured in *TIME* magazine gave Rich20. Now my job is to build on top of that. But we will never be unknown again. Number two: Inflection points can result in quantum leaps for your goals; in many cases, this is the closest you can really get to "overnight success." Case in point for us was Instagram, which was a key player in Rich20's going from five thousand to one hundred thousand subscribers in eight months. Completely unplanned, but absolutely game changing.

You know that consistency and execution are key. But you might think that consistency with your ideas will only bring slow, linear growth. That's not always the case. If you practice your craft long enough, you'll not only experience the standard linear growth, but in many cases, you'll also experience the exponential, crazy "overnight" growth of inflection points.

Some people might say that this just sounds like dumb luck, but in reality, *you need both luck (inflection points) and hard work (consistency) to reach real success.*

You MUST have both to win, no matter what order they arrive in.

If you get lucky early on in the game and blow up, you're going to need to work VERY hard to maintain that momentum; otherwise you'll see a quick spike and nothing more. And even if you're the world's hardest worker, you have to be savvy enough to recognize the inflection points when they come along; otherwise all the hard work will be for nothing.

This dynamic of consistency followed by rapid growth even occurs in nature.

Noah Kagan on Failure and Consistency

Nobody else would hire me, so I had to start my own thing. I've sacrificed a lot of time and money, but I'd 100 percent do it all over again because, for me, there's no other way. Though I have often second-guessed myself, been afraid of public rejection, and been uncertain about what my purpose really is, that's being an entrepreneur.

I'd say that I get close to giving up every eighteen months or so, because that's when I feel like moving on to the next thing. But I've persisted because of the influence of my partner, and because of my teammates, and because of the realization that all great things take time.

Noah Kagan

Founder, AppSumo

www.appsumo.com

The Strange Story of Bamboo

Bamboo is one of the most amazing plants in the world. In fact, a single stalk of bamboo has more tensile strength than a steel cable of the same thickness! In South America, it's referred to as "vegetable steel."

A rope made of bamboo fibers can get up to 20 percent stronger when wet, as opposed to hemp, which weakens. And it grows. Fast. Some species of the plant can grow a staggering three feet in a twenty-four-hour period and reach over a hundred feet in height!

It's the most rapidly growing plant on Earth. It's used for everything from construction to medicine, to cooking, to textiles. But if you were to plant a handful of bamboo seeds in the ground tomorrow, you'd be incredibly disappointed.

Why? Well, there's one HUGE problem that makes growing bamboo almost impossible for most people. And strangely enough, it's probably the same reason why 99 percent of people give up before they ever accomplish their goals.

Most people don't know that for the first five years of their lives, bamboo seedlings don't even break ground. Yes, you read that correctly. *Even with perfect care and maintenance, you won't see any progress.* You can't even be sure that they're still alive down there.

This presents many inexperienced, would-be bamboo farmers with a dilemma: They can't dig up the plants to check on them. But they're so tired of waiting for the plant to sprout, and the suspense is killing them. So what do they do? Well, the successful bamboo farmers wait patiently. Even without seeing signs of growth, they are watering their seeds. Day in, day out. Even when they're discouraged. Even when they're sure that it's futile. Then, after five years of labor and faith in something they can't see, they're rewarded with the miraculous "overnight" growth.

By the end of the week, their formerly nonexistent tree is taller than them! And of course, this begs the question: Did all that growth really happen "overnight"?

On the one hand, the apparent answer is yes. If "what you see is what you get," then all that growth happened in only a few short days. But none of that growth could have happened without the farmers' consistent action, day after day, to nurture something that was still developing—even though they couldn't see it.

Without that action, the bamboo would have died in the ground, without even a chance of sprouting.

How often do you let yourself die in the ground? How often do you get frustrated when something that you want isn't happening immediately, or at the pace that you'd like it to happen?

When we get frustrated, and we don't see the results we want, it's easy to give up. Just like the unwatered bamboo, our ambitions can die in the ground before they ever have a chance to sprout. You might think to yourself, *What's the difference? I wasn't making progress anyway.* But you'd be wrong.

First of all, you need to redefine what qualifies as "progress." Progress isn't always linear, and sometimes taking an unconventional path to your end goal means you won't be able to see every step in the staircase. But you still have to keep moving.

And remember: Sometimes you have to work at something for a long time without any apparent progress before you get a break—at which point it will seem like you've succeeded overnight. If you let negative thoughts get you down, and you stop doing the day-to-day activities that are nurturing your goals, you'll never make it.

If you quit doing the little, incremental improvements that add up to a big difference, you'll have nothing to look back on after five years.

If there's one thing to be learned from bamboo, it's that patience plus persistence (with the right things) equals growth. Remembering this on a daily basis will make it easier to push through, even when things get tough.

Quick Recap

If you're willing to be uncomfortable, and you're willing to be uncomfortable for longer than most people, something happens: You realize that you're still alive. You haven't died. You got through it. And was it really as bad as you'd built it up to be? No. So this should make you realize something else: It's OK for us to give less power to fear in our lives. We're never going to get rid of fear. And if that ever did happen, it would be disastrous. So it's time we learned how to make our own decisions rather than let fear make them for us. Fear can feel like resistance. We say things like *"I can't, because I'm scared!"* or *"I'm afraid that I'll fail."* But this resistance we feel isn't an excuse to stop—because it's actually not a red light; it's a green one. And you know what green means. Go! Use fear as a compass, not a padlock. Once you use fear as a compass, start taking action, and get yourself out there, people begin to notice. Not straightaway, but they will—if you persist. And then you'll experience an inflection point. Someone influential will share your blog post, and you'll get a ton of traffic, and that changes your business, and your life, forever. This happens ONLY if you put yourself out there and if you persist. Remember the bamboo story: You might not see any growth for five years, and then you'll see three feet of growth in one day. This is why it's important not to rely too heavily on inspiration or motivation: They're just not enough. They're great, and it's so easy to work when you're inspired and motivated, but when they desert you . . . then what? Will you be like other people and just stop working, and use the excuse *"I'm just not feeling motivated"*? Or will you remember that inspiration is for amateurs, and that it's getting to work that will get you inspired?

Notes from the Field

Ruben Chavez, Founder of ThinkGrowProsper

My friendship with Ruben is a great example of the incredible opportunity we all have to make new connections in completely unexpected, exciting ways. I would never have met him if I hadn't stumbled across his Instagram account. He has one of the biggest personal development and psychology accounts on Instagram and a legion of devoted followers who come to him for advice.

But what I like best about Ruben is he actually practices what he preaches! The genuine care and time that he puts into all the content he creates is astounding. In a world full of recycled quotes and tired catchphrases, he's always finding a way to genuinely inspire others with his insight, not just copy the work of others. He's someone I continually look to for guidance.

Check out his work at www.ThinkGrowProsper.org and on Instagram at @ThinkGrowProsper.

My "why" is all about freedom. I want freedom in terms of my time. Having a "job"—as in, having to be somewhere at a certain time until a certain time—has never appealed to me. Some jobs I liked, but it never sat well with me that I had to be there every day or I'd be fired. I was always trying to somehow fit in rather than do a custom-made role, and I wanted to change that.

I also want freedom in terms of location. I couldn't travel wherever I wanted, and I couldn't work from home whenever I wanted. Now I can.

I also want freedom from having to worry about money. I didn't grow up poor, but as soon as I was exposed to people who were living lifestyles I didn't even know were possible, I knew I wanted more in terms of finances. It's not necessarily about big houses and nice cars; it's more about not having to worry about the bills, and being able to go out to eat when I want, and being able to take my friends on holiday without worrying about how I'll pay for it. I hesitate to quote Kanye West, but something he said resonated with me: "Having money is not everything; not having it is." And he's right. It can't buy you everything, and it definitely can't buy you the intangi-

ble things, but money is nice because it helps you to have less things to worry about.

A big sacrifice I've made is not working a normal schedule. I make my own hours, but I work more for myself, and I work harder for myself, than I ever worked for anyone else. And sometimes I view this as a sacrifice, but more often than not, I view it as a privilege. Because I remember when I didn't have a choice, and I had to go to work, and I had to be there at a certain time until a certain time.

I've also sacrificed being "normal" in general. When you venture out on your own, people question you, and people don't understand you. My family has been supportive of me, but they don't get what I do. They hear things like "Instagram" and "social media entrepreneur" and they just don't understand. But I've learned now that being misunderstood comes with the territory.

The biggest excuse I made was that I couldn't succeed because I lacked resources. I didn't have money, or the right connections, and so there was no way I could be successful. This is an excuse, and a lie. I overcame it by starting small. I started the ThinkGrowProsper account on Instagram, and I had absolutely no resources, so I just focused on creating value. I started with zero capital and created a six-figure company, all because I chose to focus on giving value rather than complaining that I had no resources.

Being successful, to me, means being happy with where you are and what you have. It means being excited about what you're doing. If you're making a lot of money, but aren't excited, how successful are you? For me, it's nothing to do with money. But I will say that being excited and happy about what you're doing definitely leads to money.

If I were to go back and say something to myself on the day I started my business, I'd say this: Be OK with appealing to a specific group of people. Not everybody is your customer, and that's OK. Well, that's better than OK. Because if "everybody" is your customer, then nobody is.

I was at my closest to giving up when I quit my job, pursued an herbal supplement business, and failed. I was unemployed and I was broke. Also, my girlfriend's mother was having chemotherapy treatments at the time, and eventually she died. It was just a very challenging and dark time. But then I did something that I'd done before: I resorted to reading. I reread some old classics on success and personal development, one of which was Think and Grow Rich, by Napoleon Hill. It resonated so much with me and what I was going through that I turned some of the quotes into images and posted them on this little app I'd just discovered called Instagram. I wasn't even doing it for anyone else. I was just doing it for me. But what I was posting resonated with other people too, and then some more people, and then a lot more, and now I have an audience of well over one million followers, and that's allowed me to create a six-figure business. So if you're thinking of giving up, just remember: This is the point where everybody else will give up. And that's exactly why you must not.

PART II

The Building

How to Start a Business You
Actually Care About

6

Adapt or Die

It is not the strongest of the species that survives, nor the most intelligent that survives. It is the one that is most adaptable to change. —*Charles Darwin*

KEY TAKEAWAYS:

- $ You live in a world that is completely different from the one your parents and grandparents started working in.
- $ One stream of income isn't enough anymore.
- $ You can and should have more than one payday per month. In other words, start being a freelancer.
- $ Be aware of impostor syndrome, but know that it doesn't have to stop you or be present for your entire life.
- $ You don't need to be world class; you just need to be "good enough."
- $ Having competition for your idea means it's more likely to work, because someone else is already doing it.

ARE THERE ANY *WALKING DEAD* fans reading this right now?

I really hope so. I want to kiss each and every one of you! I LOVE THAT SHOW! If you're reading this book in 2050, please turn to your local classic TV station and begin watching it immediately!

Why do I love it so much? Surprisingly, for me, it's not the zombies. I'm not much of a horror flick guy, to be honest. Yes, it's fun to see them get their heads smooshed, but that tends to get a bit old after season six.

I love the show so much because of the *human* element. Behold, the classic postapocalyptic story line: It all begins with an incredibly deadly, highly viral disease. Over the course of the show, however, characters come to learn that while the disease and the "walkers" themselves are very dangerous, the most dangerous element of this new world isn't the zombies; it's actually the uninfected people!

In response to the absolute chaos, people become frantic. They take incredible risks. They form unlikely alliances. They commit unspeakable acts. All in the name of survival. In a dystopian world where everything has changed, staying the same as before "the crisis" means certain death for the characters in the show. They must change their thoughts, actions, and beliefs in order to survive and thrive in a more hostile environment.

And the same is true for you.

Look around you. You live in a world that is completely different from the one your parents and grandparents inherited. That's especially true when we're talking about making a living. The path laid out before us isn't quite so simple anymore.

At this point, it's "adapt or die." Playing by the old rules will get you killed. OK, I lied. If you don't adapt to the new world order, it's unlikely somebody is *actually* going to kill you. But continuing to play this new game with an old strategy WILL leave you broke. That's a fact.

What might *actually* kill you is the lack of fulfillment that you get from not having the experiences, people, and things you want in your life. And guess what? More money can help solve this problem.

Let me lay it out for you, plain and simple: *In the new economy, you need to make more money than before to do the things you want to do.* Period.

One stream of income simply isn't enough anymore. The world is too expensive, our tastes are evolving with each generation, and in order to get what we want, we need more resources. And if you're perfectly happy with the amount of money you make now, imagine how many other people you could help if you made more. Money is important.

"OK, Captain Obvious, tell me something I don't know."

Now, lest you think I'm going all Gordon Gekko on you, hear me out: Money is not the be-all and end-all. Money won't make you feel loved or accepted. It won't turn back time and make your mom hug you more. It will not solve deep-seated personal issues or make you feel like you're "good enough" if you've always struggled with self-worth. It won't kick your high school bully's ass. Money can't force you to stop eating McDonald's or tell you to go to bed earlier. It kinda just sits there and looks at you.

But money CAN open doors for you. It can fly you out for a long weekend to see your family in another state or another country. Money can take care of not only your bills but the bills of people you care about, and can relieve the stress of paycheck-to-paycheck living.

It can buy you a nicer wardrobe that will help boost your self-esteem. Money can take you and five friends out to dinner and pay for appetizers (and drinks) without your worrying about how the bill is going to be split when the check comes.

Money is the power to do things. Money is fun. You need more of it.

Building Multiple Income Streams with Freelancing

Somewhere along the way of "traditional" career development, we were led to believe that our paycheck should be our only source of income. The paycheck comes once or twice a month in most cases and is typically associated with how many hours we are working in a specific location on a variety of tasks (these tasks, taken together, equate to your "job").

And since most of us take home only one or two paychecks a month, we've also been conditioned to believe that our paychecks should come from only one employer—one big granddaddy company that breaks off a little crumb for us to nibble on every few weeks. Mmm, yum.

But hold on to your seat and let me blow your mind: *You can and should have MORE than one or two paydays every month. And you should be making money from more than one source.*

Gasp! *"Oh no, he di'inttttttt!"*

It's not that radical an idea if you really think about it. Cars come with spare tires in the trunk. Parachutes come with emergency chutes, just in case. Hell, some shirts come with backup buttons. Yet we depend on a single source of income to provide for ourselves and our family?

It just doesn't make sense!

So why don't most people have more than one source of income? Yes, plenty of really hardworking people have second jobs—and that's great. But what I'm talking about here is significantly different. I'm talking about freelancing.

What is freelancing?

Freelancing is all about building a side hustle with a skill, hobby, or ability that you already have and monetizing your expertise. In my advanced course Freelance Domination 2.0, we have freelancers in all disciplines, from all areas of the globe. (You can learn more about Freelance Domination 2.0 at www.Rich20Something.com/bonus.)

My students are successfully turning their skills, ideas, and talents into significant income by providing a wide range of services, from web design to consulting to dog walking. The possibilities are endless! The money from your side business can be scaled up or dialed back at will and in direct response to your needs, and it can be directed wherever you want.

You can hoard that income like a greedy Scrooge McDuck, or you can spend it at your discretion on things that are important to you: a long weekend trip, a Hugo Boss jacket, all seven appetizers on the menu next time you go to Chili's— your pick. Developing a small, powerful freelance business will open up the doors to financial freedom and give you skills you can immediately apply as you travel further on the road to success.

Now here are two really cool things about having a side business that most people don't know:

1. You don't have to quit your job if you don't want to.
2. You don't have to work double the number of hours you're already working in order to make two times, three times, or even five times the amount of money you're making at your nine-to-five.

Quick clarification here: I'm not one of those breathe-down-your-neck entrepreneur evangelists who believe everyone on Earth should be a full-time, self-employed workaholic. Yes, I think that starting your own business is the most logical way to create the life that you want. But I also recognize that some people actually ENJOY their jobs.

Shocker, right? Sometimes working for an interesting company provides you with an opportunity to do things as part of a team that you just wouldn't be able to do by yourself—and I'm not hatin' on that! (For instance, I always thought working for Elon Musk at Tesla or SpaceX would be really fun! Can anybody get me a job there? Call me!)

That being said, you can absolutely start freelancing while working full-time and scale it up depending on your needs and preferences. Need to make a bit more money? Scale it up. Need more time for your nine-to-five or other creative projects? Put it on ice for a bit.

And if you ever want to leave your current job, you can gradually ratchet it up to match (then exceed) your income without missing a beat—or a paycheck. It's the ultimate freedom. Now, here's where it gets tricky: If you search online for "how to start a side business" or "how to start a freelance business," you're likely going to get a lot of conflicting advice.

To test my theory, I just searched both of these search terms on Google. One of the top results was a list of 130-plus side business ideas.

Among them were some gems, such as:

- Filling out online surveys. (Shoot me in the brain right now. Seriously. Shoot me.)
- Collecting art. (This doesn't seem like something that can be done quickly, or with less than a million dollars liquid. Just sayin'.)
- Human billboard. (I guess if you're already giving out dick pics for free, you might as well get paid?)

Not exactly what I'd call helpful ideas. There were also some good ideas in the list, don't get me wrong. My main concern is not about coming up with ideas—at least not at this stage.

People get tripped up on finding the perfect idea, but in reality, their good idea is worthless without understanding the foundation and mechanics necessary to actually start and grow a business. Once you understand the process for how to start and grow a freelance business from the ground up on a high level, you can take any idea from zero to twenty thousand, fifty thousand, or even a hundred thousand dollars or more using the same framework over and over again.

Everything becomes "plug and play." I've done this with multiple freelance businesses, and I'll show you exactly how to replicate (and even exceed) my results!

Dealing with Mental Barriers to Success

Starting any type of business (even if it's just a small side hustle) always seems scary in the beginning because as a novice, you can't accurately interpret the amount of risk involved. You exaggerate the potential severity of failures that haven't even happened yet, then wrap yourself in the emotions you'd feel if they were to happen.

You read statistics online that say 90 percent of all businesses fail, and you automatically lump yourself in with that majority. At the forefront of your mind, several key mental barriers are probably popping up.

If you don't have any doubts or fears about your abilities, you're, like, weird. Or you're lying. Everyone does. I did. People who are much more successful than I am did as well. This is a normal part of your evolution that can't and shouldn't be avoided, but should instead be dealt with.

The purpose of a mental barrier is to "protect" you. These barriers will continue to surface throughout your entrepreneurial journey. It's your subconscious mind's attempt to shield you from high-risk, potentially harmful situations, or situations that could damage your ego.

These barriers will keep weighing you down and stalling the progress of your side business. Until you deal with them head-on, they'll cripple you and make it extremely difficult to succeed.

Let's deal with them right here, right now, and move past them once and for all.

Mental barrier: Perceived lack of experience, expertise, or ability

Sounds like: *Why would anybody listen to me/help me/pay me?* or *I'm not good enough.*

If you can overcome only one barrier on the road to success, this is the one you should focus on. Here's a little secret: Nearly everyone feels incompetent at what they do for some period of time. Sometimes this feeling of incompetence goes on for years—or indefinitely. We don't feel like we're talented enough, capable enough, or experienced enough to "deserve" compensation for our efforts.

Closely related is "impostor syndrome," a psychological state in which world-class experts fail to recognize their own accomplishments and are constantly worried about being exposed as a fraud. For example, in a recent interview with Emma Watson, the beautiful, megasuccessful actress confessed, *"Any moment, someone's going to find out I'm a total fraud . . . I can't possibly live up to what everyone thinks I am."* Pretty fucked up, huh?

If mental barriers like this are a huge problem for people who have already seen massive success, what does that mean for the rest of us who are still on our journey and have yet to taste any real victory? It can be incredibly hard to believe that you're good enough, that you're worth it.

Here's the way I like to think about it: You don't need to be an "expert" with years of experience to start turning your skills and ideas into money. In some instances, you just need to be willing to learn as you go. *This means that if you can help people get results faster than they would get them alone, that is more than enough reason to charge for the service.*

My favorite example of this concept is learning to ride a

bike. If you're like most of us, you were probably taught to ride your first bike by a sibling or older family member. You wanted so badly to just get on the thing and fly, but you needed help from someone who'd already done it before. When your older sibling offered to teach you, did you stop him and say, *"Excuse me, are you a professional cyclist? How many Tour de Frances have you won?"*

OF COURSE NOT! All you could think about was riding down the block, and you knew he could help you get there much faster than you could trying to figure it out yourself— even though he wasn't an "expert" bike rider.

And when you finally stumbled your way to the end of the street without falling, I bet you were immensely grateful that your sibling was gracious enough to share his knowledge. He just saved you a few scraped knees!

The take-home here is that it's perfectly OK to help people with something and get paid for it, even if you are still developing a skill or you're not an expert. All businesses are about problem-solving, which means that *as long as you can help the person get results faster with you than without you, you deserve to get paid!* **You don't need to be world class—just "good enough."**

IRA GLASS, radio personality and host and producer of the enormously popular show *This American Life*, has some profound observations for those of us who are in the beginning stages of creative careers—especially with regard to the inevitable feelings of inadequacy that plague even very talented people:

*Nobody tells people who are beginners—and I really wish some-
body had told this to me—is that all of us who do creative
work . . . we get into it because we have good taste. But it's like
there's a gap, that for the first couple years that you're making
stuff, what you're making isn't so good. . . . It's not that great. It's
trying to be good, it has ambition to be good, but it's not quite
that good. But your taste—the thing that got you into the
game—your taste is still killer, and your taste is good enough
that you can tell that what you're making is kind of a disappoint-
ment to you. . . . A lot of people never get past that phase. A lot of
people, at that point, they quit. . . . Most everybody I know who
does interesting, creative work, they went through a phase of
years where . . . they knew it fell short, it didn't have the special
thing that we wanted it to have. . . . Everybody goes through that.
And for you to go through it, if you're going through it right now,
if you're just getting out of that phase—you gotta know it's totally
normal. And the most important possible thing you can do is do
a lot of work. . . . Put yourself on a deadline so that every week, or
every month, you know you're going to finish one story. Because
it's only by actually going through a volume of work that you are
actually going to catch up and close that gap. And the work
you're making will be as good as your ambitions. It takes a
while . . . and you just have to fight your way through that.*

Reading that again, I can't help but think about my feelings when writing this book. I really want it to be good. I
hope it is. Hopefully the hundreds of articles and blog posts
I've written up to this point have shaped my work enough to
give it the unique voice I always heard in my head but often
struggled to translate into words.

If this Google doc makes it off my computer and into bookstores (and your precious hands), you'll know I succeeded. But it took time and a LOT of crappy work in between.

Mental barrier: Perceived lack of originality or uniqueness in your idea

Sounds like: *Wahhhh! Other people are already doing what I want to do!*

This one makes me laugh! Think about it: If lack of originality were a real barrier to entry in a marketplace, there wouldn't be more than one of anything. Imagine if Apple decided not to start a computer company because IBM was already in business before them. Ridiculous!

Do you remember a search engine called AltaVista? Yeah, most people don't. It was one of the first to get popular back in 1995, but was eventually overtaken by competitors. What if Google had decided not to go into business because there was already somebody doing what they wanted to do?

Life without variety sucks, and oftentimes customers will buy from both you *and* your competitors multiple times. I have an Apple Watch, a Fitbit, and a Pavlok—three separate wearable devices that serve different purposes—and I love them all.

Think about it this way: Competition means that your business idea is more likely to work, since if it's working for someone else, it can probably work for you too.

We'll discuss the nuances of this in depth, plus how to stand out from the competition, in the next chapter. For now, remember this: It doesn't matter if someone else is already doing what you want to do. If you can do it differently or better, you can carve out a spot for yourself, even in a very crowded market.

Quick Recap

The world of today is very different from the world that your parents and grandparents lived in. For example, things are more expensive. And we want more things. And we need more things, honestly: Did your parents or grandparents have mobile phones or laptops or an Apple Watch? Obviously, there's something that can help with this: money. We know that money won't solve all our problems, or make us feel "good enough," but it can make things happen.

So how do you make more money? One word: freelancing. And this is how you can have more than one payday per month. Who doesn't want more than one payday per month? If and when you start freelancing, some interesting feelings might come up: feelings that you're not good enough at what you're doing, feelings that there's already plenty of competition out there for your idea. These feelings are essentially symptoms of impostor syndrome, a syndrome where even world-class experts fear others will discover that they're complete frauds. But here's the good news: You don't need to be world class to make money from freelancing. Far from it. And if there's already competition out there for your idea, that means your idea will probably work.

Notes from the Field

Steven Mehr, CEO of Webshark360 and Chairman of Jacoby & Meyers

Steven is one of the rarest people I know. We met in Las Vegas at an Instagram "influencers" meetup and, in a strange turn of events, ended up driving back together from Vegas to LA when a storm grounded our flights. It was during that ride that I got to know him, and I will say this: Not often do you meet someone who's able to evenly balance humility with massive success, but he's mastered it. And the most interesting part is that he started from nothing and built a multi-multimillion-dollar empire in multiple disciplines.

What you'll find is that his success didn't revolve around luck. It revolved around discipline and patience, combined with a sense of urgency. If I ask Steven to get something done, that shit gets done!

I'm proud to call him a friend.

You can find out more about him at www.SteveMehr .com and at @AgentSteven on Instagram.

I'm the CEO of a media company, a chairman of a law office, a start-up investor, a real estate investor, and I teach other entrepreneurs about how to be a successful entrepreneur. My first business was selling shoelaces, and I'd sell them for one dollar a pair. Then, one Christmas, I returned the Christmas gifts I'd received so I could buy some speakers and sell them to the rich kids at school. I did that, and eventually I was making between five thousand and ten thousand dollars a month selling audio equipment to schoolkids in the area.

It was difficult for me when I told my parents I didn't want to go to college. They were immigrants, and for immigrants to turn down a chance at education was unheard of. But I didn't want to continue with my education. I wanted to continue running my business, and to open up an actual brick-and-mortar store. But I ran into a problem: Nobody would give a load of money to an eighteen-year-old kid so he could open a store. So I made a deal with my dad: He'd give me the money as long as I went to college and studied law.

And that's what I did. For seven years, I worked seven days a week and took my college classes at night. Friday nights, while my friends were out partying and getting laid, I was either sleeping because I was exhausted or I was working on my law degree. It's easy to talk about making sacrifices, and it's a fashionable thing right now in being an entrepreneur, but I just don't see people doing it. I also sacrificed having any kind of stable girlfriend, any real free time, seeing my friends, because my dreams were that important to me. They were important to me, and I acted like they were important to me.

I also made sacrifices because I wanted a certain kind of lifestyle. My parents provided well for me, but I wanted to buy things they'd never be able to buy me. So my motivation for making money, when I first started out, was quite shallow. It was all about me and what I wanted.

That was, until I realized that money just makes you more of who you are. And I'd never been greedy when it came to money; I'd only ever been greedy when it came to my time. Lots of people still tell me now that it's selfish and greedy and shallow to make lots of money. Well, this Thanksgiving, I'm aiming to be able to feed ten thousand families. Is that selfish or greedy or shallow? I live my life by putting myself first so that I can get ahead, because then I'll be able to impact more people and bring more people with me. People talk about doing social work in order to help people and to give back; well, if I put myself first and I make a lot of money, I can start my own orphanage. That's real social work.

Being successful, to me, is being able to live life on my own terms, and to be free of "normal" constraints. And before you're able to do this, you have to hustle. You have to work seven days a week for seven years, like I did. You can't just skip that step and have your life set up exactly how you want it. You're not entitled to that. What you do have is the opportunity to earn that.

I earned that by saying yes to all the opportunities that came my way when I was first starting out. I said yes because opportunities weren't coming my way. Why would they be? I'd just started out. So anything I got offered, I said yes to, because I wanted to capitalize on everything, no matter how big or small. Now that I've had some success, I've had to get really good at saying no. It's a strange transition, going from saying yes all the time to saying no all the time.

Now, I create time in my day by ignoring 90 percent of what happens, and I do that because only 10 percent of what happens even matters anyway. I firmly believe this: You cannot be reactive. You have to be conscious of being reactive, and you have to choose not to be, and you have to instead be proactive. You have to be the one choosing how you spend your day, not someone else.

And that's why you have to ask yourself this question: Does doing this thing bring me closer to my goal? And then you have to answer it in a binary way: yes or no. It either brings you closer to your goal or it doesn't. And if it doesn't, you mustn't do it. If it does, then you must do it. Simple, but not easy, and it takes a lot of practice. But this is how you become effective rather than productive.

I prefer to be effective rather than productive because being productive could mean that I'm getting lots of things done but that none of them really, truly matter. What's the point in that? Being effective—that's how to spend your time. Pick the one thing you need to do to move forward, and spend your time on that. Notice I didn't say two things, or three things. One thing. Think how much quicker you'd move forward if you just focused on one thing, day in and day out.

To any entrepreneurs out there who have only just started, or who are struggling, I say this: Some pear trees take seven years to bear fruit. Seven years! Even after taking care of one for six years, watering it, giving it sun, feeding it: nothing. No signs of success whatsoever. This is like being an entrepreneur. I see too many people give up *too soon because they're not willing to be patient. They want it all now, and they forget that it doesn't work like that. They forget that being an entrepreneur is like the pear tree.*

So with that in mind, the more patient you can be, the bigger the competitive advantage you'll have. And you'll have an even bigger one if you combine patience with a sense of urgency.

7

Hustling 101: How to Make $100,000 Freelancing

There's no such thing as being too independent.
—*Victoria Billings*

KEY TAKEAWAYS:

$ Freelancing is the bridge between your nine-to-five and true independence.

$ Starting a business is not as risky as the media makes it out to be.

$ The Three-Question Validation: Is there competition in my space? Are my competitors making money? Can I do my idea differently and/or better?

$ The Marsupial Method works best: Find other, more established businesses, and then create win-win-win scenarios that add value to their business, to their customers, and to yourself.

$ Do free work and give incredible value.

NOW THAT WE'VE DISCUSSED some of the roadblocks you're likely to encounter, let's dive in.

Freelancing is an essential skill set that will serve you well for the rest of your life. Once you develop the ability to quickly come up with a good idea, find people who want to buy from you, and consistently sell yourself, you'll never be in danger of becoming unemployed again.

You will be the master of your destiny, with complete control over how much you get paid for your time—and by extension, the level of lifestyle you want to live.

In many cases, you'll also be able to build up your credibility in your field and become an authority in your space. This type of exposure can help build a substantial personal brand and open doors to all types of opportunity.

Freelancing is the bridge between your nine-to-five and true independence.

Two quick notes before we talk tactics:

1. The goal with your first freelance business doesn't have to be finding your ultimate passion. This isn't like picking a major in college. If you try it out and decide you don't like it, you can always switch classes. As your interests evolve over time, you'll naturally lean toward things that excite you the most.

2. You don't need a million-dollar idea. You don't need to reinvent Google or make "Facebook for dogs." You just need a one-dollar idea. If you can find an idea that someone will pay one dollar for, you can convince her to pay ten dollars, then a hundred, then eventually a thousand. There's no need to be fancy here. The highest-paid freelancers are the ones who do something simple and specialized, and who do it extremely well.

How to Find a Business Idea That's Guaranteed to Work

The main reason businesses fail isn't because business itself is "too hard." The media (especially social media) would have you think that starting a successful business was akin to becoming a chess grand master or discovering alchemy.

Chill out.

Starting a successful business is hard, but it's not any harder than the more "traditional" and socially acceptable things that most people are comfortable undertaking—like medical school, for instance. Many people are happy to rush to apply to med school because it seems straightforward and secure. Doctors make money, so just do this and you'll be OK. Right?

But think about the medical school process . . . Just to get your foot in the door, you need to pass a variety of rigorous tests to prove your merit. If you're not serious about the field and extremely committed to learning, you won't even make it past this stage. Then you have to spend upward of six years (on top of the four you already spent in undergraduate school) developing your ideas and learning how to identify, neutralize, and heal countless different ailments in a high-stress environment.

Professors will criticize and scrutinize your work. There's a ton of competition for a limited amount of attention, grants, and resources. The entire process is grotesquely expensive: According to *Inc.* magazine, the median cost of the typical four-year private medical school in the United States was $278,000 in 2013.

None of these expenses include the typical three- to four-year period of "residency" that is required for specializations such as internal medicine. (Neurosurgeons spend an additional seven years in residency after med school, bringing their total to eleven years.) That's what I call *expensive*—both in time and money!

Many new physicians come out of school saddled with almost four hundred thousand dollars in debt and hardly a hope of paying it off anytime soon, even with salaries well above average. I don't know about you, but this proposition seems extremely risky to me. Yet the world tells us that this is a "safe" path. Seems a bit skewed, don't you think?

Do we need more doctors? Absolutely. I encourage people to become physicians! The world is a better place for it. But let's not presume that entrepreneurship itself is intrinsically riskier (or scarier) than those things that popular culture deems "acceptable." Next time someone on your Facebook timeline spouts off about how risky it is to start a business, just remember that everything worth doing comes with some inherent risk.

You'll never be able to completely avoid risk, either in your personal or professional life. But you can mitigate it significantly by having a solid game plan in place. You need a proven system that will help you determine which ideas are worth pursuing so that you don't become a statistic of America, Inc.

You want to be as certain as possible that your business will succeed BEFORE you launch. In other words, you need to "failproof" it. And luckily for you, I've developed a process to get you as close to 100 percent sure as humanly possible. It's called **Three-Question Validation**, and we'll go over this method step-by-step. I'll give you a sample business idea and show you how this process would be used to make sure the idea is failproof; then we'll work our way back to the drawing board to help you come up with a kick-ass idea.

How to Failproof Your Idea with Three-Question Validation

At its core, Three-Question Validation involves asking yourself three pivotal questions to determine if your business idea is viable and likely to succeed. It's a compact method to test if your idea holds water before you waste the time, energy, and money on something that isn't going to work. If you *can* say yes to all three of them, you have an idea that's likely to do very well. If you *can't* say yes to all of them, it's time to go back to the drawing board.

Question 1: "Is there competition in my space?"
We addressed this quickly in the chapter 5 section about overcoming doubts, but it's worth circling back to. Contrary to popular belief, you WANT competitors in your space.

If you find a market that's 100 percent unoccupied, you're either the first one there (risky, in that nothing has been tested) or the last one there (other people have tried unsuccessfully and abandoned the market).

Being the first isn't horrible, but there's less of a road map to follow.

Being last doesn't mean that you can't find a way to make your idea work in the marketplace, but rather that it will take considerably more work.

Remember, the purpose of this freelance business doesn't have to be finding the number one thing you want to do for the rest of your life. It's a bridge to freedom. It's a tool to bring in some more money as you get the rest of your life in order. Over time, you may find other things you like more, and that's totally OK.

For now, let's try to pick something that has a high probability of succeeding so that you can build your confidence, business savvy, and skill set.

Pick something where there appears to be many other people doing what you'd like to do. If you can answer yes to this question, it's time to move on to the next question.

Question 2: "Are my competitors making money?"
A bit of a no-brainer, but very important to consider: Even if there are people doing what you want to do, you need to make sure they have enough clients and are making the type of money you'd like to make.

This step will ensure that it's worth your time to invest in your idea. There are a bunch of different ways to tell how well your competition is doing. You could look on their website for testimonials and client success stories. Browse through their portfolio if they have one. You could stop in (if they are local) and talk to them, or give them a call over the phone. Ask about rates, schedule, and typical client experience. Obviously don't tell them why you're doing this research.

I love looking at unbiased third-party sites like Yelp and checking to see what a competitor's rating is and what customers have to say. You don't need to get exact revenue numbers. The point here is just to get a general sense of how they're doing.

If other people are successfully getting clients and customers, so can you.

Question 3: "Can I do my product/service/idea differently and/or better?"

This is the question that ties everything together. You've found your competition. They appear to have some business. Now what?

It's time to make your stand by standing out.

In order for customers to buy your idea over another company's (or in addition to theirs), you must show why your product or service is different and/or better. If you can show how you're unique, you'll attract just the right customers who are perfect for your business. The type of clients who will buy from you time and again, and who will continually refer you to all their friends.

This point of difference between you and your competition is called USP, short for "unique selling proposition."

Here are five examples of how to stand out with a USP:

1. **Better (lower) price.** Typically, I don't like competing on price; I prefer to provide greater value and get paid accordingly. However, when you're just getting started and you're not 100 percent confident in your skills, it may behoove you to have a lower price point than more experienced competitors. You won't have to stay there forever as long as you increase the value of your services, but under-

cutting your competition and then providing stellar work will help to get your first few customers in the door. And they'll bring their friends. There's a reason why Walmart continues to lead the retail game. Everybody knows that their USP is "Always Low Prices." Again, I want to stress that the quality of your work still needs to be very high. That's key, since most people expect that lower prices equate to lower-quality work. Blow their expectations out of the water and you'll most certainly draw attention, recognition, and a steady stream of new business.

2. **Convenience.** Making your products or services more convenient for the customer to use or access gives you a huge advantage. As a society, we're used to getting things not just now but RIGHT NOW. I'm calling it the "Uberization" of the world. A few weeks ago, I ordered a Fitbit to track my sleeping patterns. Amazon shipped and delivered it the same day. It was on my wrist by seven o'clock that night, just in time to start logging my sleep. You can take advantage of this trend by making your products and services extremely simple to access.

One of my Freelance Domination 2.0 students, Micah, is a personal trainer. But rather than have clients come to him, he makes the process EXTREMELY easy on them. Micah's gym is mobile. He bought one of those old white vans and wrapped it in a giant sticker with his face and logo. Every morning, at your appointment time, he shows up to your door, pulls you out of bed, and works you out. You don't even need to change out of your pajamas if you don't want to. All the equipment is in the van already: weights, resistance bands, kettlebells. After your session, he provides a healthy snack. Because working out with him is so much easier than getting dressed, fighting traffic, and dragging yourself to the gym, clients are flocking to him and he can charge increasingly higher rates than his competitors. Convenience pays.

3. **Better quality or aesthetic.** In my house I have two MacBooks, an iPad, a twenty-seven-inch iMac desktop, two iPhones, and an Apple Watch. And I don't even own Apple stock. (Seriously rethinking that right about now.)

I also don't consider myself a diehard Apple fanboy. But I DO love the way all my technology looks. Despite arguably slipping a few points every year in their technological advancement, there's one thing Apple does really well: make beautiful products that don't break easily or often.

The quality and attention to detail you put into your products and services are huge factors in a customer's buying decision. If it looks or performs better than the competition, I'm more likely to buy. That's just basic human psychology. (It's also a good way to pick a girlfriend. But that's another book.)

4. **More variety.** Did you ever see that Subway commercial where they touted that you could make over a thousand different sandwiches?

As an ex-SAT instructor, I'm somewhat irked by it, as it's simply basic multiplication of toppings, not an indicator of sandwich superiority. But the campaign was highly effective.

In a world where everything is instantaneous, we want to get started quickly and have the MAXIMUM amount of flexibility in our choices. If you can provide that, you can stand out!

5. **Superior customer service or guarantee.** Most competitors in your space are going to have average or below-average customer service. They'll get back to people "soon-ish" but with no urgency.

   They'll offer refunds or exchange policies, but only ones that are designed to protect the company's best interests, not the customers.

   There's a huge opportunity here for you to rise above and provide first-class service and a better overall experience.

   If your competition provides a 30-day money-back guarantee, make yours 60 days . . . or 180! If they usually respond to clients in one business day, make it a point to respond to any inquiries the same day in four hours or less.

   There's a certain medical marijuana delivery service in Los Angeles that I've absolutely never used. They offer service from eleven o'clock in the morning to eleven at night, 365 days a year. Their competitors are always closed or busy. You know who I'd hypothetically call when I wanted to get blazed on a Friday night? Exactly!

   Customer service, people!

   These seemingly small tweaks to your offer are big in your customers' minds, and really add up over time. In addition, they are free or at least cheap to implement, so there's really no reason not to! It's such a low-hanging fruit if you want to stand out!

Alexandra Wolf on Starting Out

There was a point where I didn't think that anyone would care about what I had to offer. But it was only once I owned the information that I was providing, even if it wasn't necessarily that advanced, that my business took off.

I persisted because I think it's a bigger risk to not pursue your dreams than it is to pursue them. What else was I going to do—settle for plan B?

The first thing you should do when starting your business is to get an actual customer. Think about everything else afterward. It's like Seth Godin said: You're not entitled to demand. You have to try to create it. The market will decide if there's demand for your product.

Alexandra Wolf

Founder, Boss Babe Academy (the number one personal branding
*   school for millennial women)*

www.Bossbabe.me

Three-Question Validation in Action
Tactical Example

Throughout this process, I'm going to continually emphasize the fact that almost ANY idea or skill can be made into a profitable freelance side business. (When I say "almost any," I'm leaving a small margin of error for stupid ideas. Sorry, freelance beaver therapists and independent ice-cream consultants!)

So let's run through a few different examples in different fields and try them out using the Three-Question Validation method. I want you to see how flexible but accurate this methodology is.

Becoming a "Personal Shopper"

Let's look at an unconventional example. Let's say you LOVE shopping and fashion. You love going to the mall and trying on things, even if you're not buying. You love looking through magazines and dreaming up new looks for yourself and your friends. Maybe you get lots of compliments on how you dress and style yourself. How do you take this idea from an expensive hobby into a business that actually pays you money?

I'll show you a very simple way to tell if your idea is even a business—and if that business is good enough to pursue. It all starts with the three questions.

Question 1: "Is there competition in my space?"

The counterintuitive logic here: Most people spend countless hours trying to think of an original idea. They spend hours and hours trying to figure out something that's completely unique. It's the lure of uncharted territory, baby!

THIS IS ONE OF THE BIGGEST MISTAKES YOU CAN MAKE.

Why? When you're first starting out, your only goal is to make money. We're not trying to revolutionize an industry here. We're not trying to wow venture capitalists with our space-age solution. We simply want to know what works, and we can hedge a TON of risk by looking at what others are already doing.

The easiest way to figure out this piece of the puzzle is simply to google it. In our example above, let's say you wanted to be a personal stylist and get paid to help people find and build an awesome wardrobe. Is there anybody doing this already? Let's check . . .

I ran a local search for "personal shopper Santa Monica," and some VERY interesting results popped up:

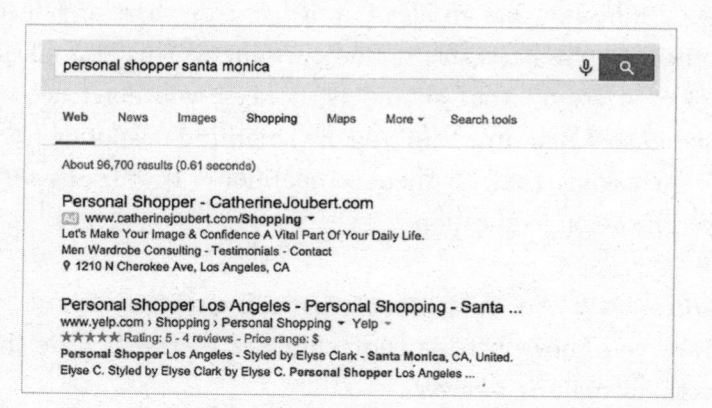

Wow . . . 96,700 results. Are any of them relevant, though?

So check this out: There were a TON of results. Even looking at the first two, I see some very interesting indicators:

- Someone (Catherine Joubert, apparently) is paying to have her ad placed for this search term. She's spending money to advertise, which tells me there's a good chance she's making money doing this.
- The first result is for a Yelp page, which lists not just one but several different personal shoppers in the area. In Yelp alone, there are seventy-seven pages of personal stylists in LA/Santa Monica.

Whoa. Suddenly we went from, "Can I even get paid for my interest in fashion?" to "How the hell am I supposed to stand out?"

But we have answered our key question: There is DEFI-NITELY competition.

Getting into an already saturated market can be a good thing, if you know what you're doing. A saturated market is a good indicator that an idea is worthy, since there are clearly others who've been able to find customers. This also takes a lot of stress off your shoulders, because you don't need to spend so much time thinking of something revolutionary.

So ask yourself, "Is there competition?" If your answer is yes, move on to question 2.

Question 2: "Are my competitors making money?"

Now you know that the competition is there—but are they actually making money?

Let's go back to the results from the search we just did. Here's what one stylist's search results looked like:

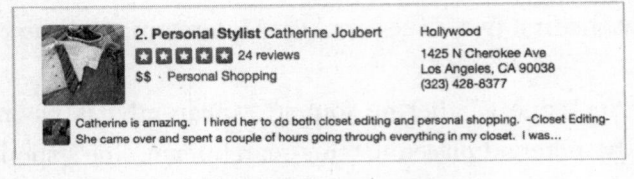

More than fifty reviews! Nice!

This has gotten more than fifty reviews on Yelp—which is quite a lot, considering that 98 percent of people will prob-ably NEVER leave a review, even if they love your service.

(We're all busy, lazy, forgetful, etc.) This means she's probably had quite a few clients, since these are just the people who stopped by to leave a review. Then, when you click on her profile, the reviews are incredibly positive and highly recommend her. Nice job, Catherine!

This is all great news for you too, future stylist. You can see now that it's possible to get LOTS of clients, and it appears Catherine is making money. She's not the only one. Several of the other stylists from the same search have over a dozen reviews and many satisfied customers.

If you can find evidence that your competitors are getting clients and making money, you can answer yes to question 2.

A quick note here: You may not want to do a local-based business or something that has Yelp reviews. That's fine. You'll still take the same steps of researching your competition, seeing what they're doing, and determining if they have clients. Don't get caught up on the particulars of this example; think big picture.

Now we're on to question 3 . . .

Question 3: "Can I do my product/service/idea differently and/or better?"

At this point, you know that your idea is viable and it'll make money, but you need to stand out from the pack in order to make a dent—especially if the field is particularly crowded. Again, research is your friend here. First, you need to identify which needs in your market are going unfulfilled, then deliver a service that caters to those specific holes.

For example, a few positions you could use to stand out are:

- Better prices
- Convenience (closer, easier to access, quicker to implement, etc.)
- Aesthetics
- Exclusivity/scarcity/status symbol
- More customized service
- Better-quality product
- Better selection, always in stock, etc.
- Being "trendier" or more cutting-edge
- Better customer support
- Faster service
- Better warranty or guarantee

These are a few examples, and if you want more, I put together an entire cheat sheet for you to download that will tell you exactly how to come up with ideas that will stand out. You can grab it at www.Rich20Something.com/bonus.

How to Find Your Profitable Idea

Before we go any further, I have one favor to ask of you: Don't start freaking out, OK?

Most people get really weird or anxious when it's time to start developing ideas for their business. It almost gets a bit "meta" at times. Why? Lots of people love the idea of brainstorming ideas, but can never actually find an idea that they like enough to execute. Or often, they don't think it's "good enough" to execute. I'm not sure why or how, but as soon as we think of a potential business idea, most of us seem to get this bug that makes us believe whatever we think of isn't "good enough." Potential or aspiring entrepreneurs seem to face two huge problems when it comes to developing an idea:

1. **We don't think we have any good ideas**, so there's nothing we can possibly see succeeding. This is the guy who's always telling you about a new project he wants to start, and then you find out two weeks later he's already completely abandoned it.
2. **We think we have too many good ideas**, and we are completely confused as to which one we should run with long-term. This is the guy who always has twelve projects brewing at the same time, all in various stages of progress, none really doing well.

While these seem to be opposing concepts, they often ensnare us in the same dilemma: half-starting and eventually quitting.

So where SHOULD you be focusing your time and energy? How do you know if your idea is good enough to "make it"?

First, remember two things:

1. As I said before, you don't need a million-dollar idea. This is VERY important to keep in mind, as it's very easy to feel like we need to be thinking BIGGER in the beginning.

What I'm telling you to do is to think a bit smaller—at least at first. Case in point: If you look at high-level competitive martial artists, you'll see that even the most spectacular wins are usually the result of world-class fundamentals. Even against elite competition, doing the basics uncommonly well is usually more than enough to come out on top.

If you can master doing simple things really well right now, you'll still make a ton of money AND prepare yourself for more advanced things later.

2. All businesses—services and products, online or offline—are a direct response to a problem. The purpose of a business—the only reason it exists, in fact—is to solve a problem.

You should be actively thinking of how you can solve other people's problems. On a day-to-day basis, you should be thinking about things you and others around you struggle with, then finding ways to solve those headaches through an idea, device, service, or piece of software. Better yet, start pretending you're Olivia Pope and become relentless in your approach to problem-solving and "fixing" things.

Coming up with fresh business ideas shouldn't be something that you do just once a year when you need some money. If you want to be an entrepreneur, you must fundamentally change the way you look at the world, always seeking out opportunities to serve other people and get paid in return. With this in mind, your well of creative inspiration will never run dry.

Here are four places I look first when I want to come up with a new business idea quickly:

1. **Things you're already good at (hobbies/skills).** Everybody has SOMETHING that they're good at. The problem is, most of us take our skills for granted. We don't appreciate the

fact that the knowledge and abilities we have at our disposal could be very valuable to someone else:

- Maybe you're bilingual or you can play an instrument.
- Perhaps you know how to organize the HELL out of a closet.
- Maybe you're really good at cooking, or building websites.
- You might have even successfully completed a few triathlons.

All of these are things that other people would like to be able to do for themselves on a regular basis but in many cases can't.

Understand this: TIME is the only real commodity we have. We make money so that we can pay other people to do things for us in order to gain more time. It all comes back to time.

If you've spent considerable time learning to do something—either in school, as an apprentice, or even as a hobby or recreational activity—that time has immense value. Rather than learning to do what you've done or putting in months (or years) of work grinding away, many people will be more than happy to pay you in order to get what they want much more quickly. You can teach someone else how to do something. Or, if you don't want to teach it, you can simply use that skill to provide a service and do the work for them.

2. **Things you've done for work**. SPOILER ALERT: "Learned at work" skills are a great place to look when fishing for your first profitable business idea. If you've ever held a job, that's proof you have at least one skill or idea that somebody will be willing to pay money for!

Like most people, you may be under the assumption that your hourly wage or salary reflects the actual value of your skills, but here's the thing: There is no "actual" or innate value of a skill, service, or idea:

- Washing dishes could be a seven-dollar-an-hour skill or a fifteen-dollar-an-hour skill, depending on whose plates you're cleaning.
- Building a mobile app for your employer could be one of the hundreds of other things you do every year as part of your sixty-thousand-dollar salary.
- Or the same mobile app could be a twenty-thousand-dollar side project that you work on in your free time, while still making sixty thousand at work.

Your salary doesn't reflect true value; it just reflects your employer's estimation of how much they can afford to pay you after they've accounted for all their expenses and made a healthy profit. If you have a boss, you're not making as much money as you could be for your time. Period.

Here's a partial list of all the things taking money out of your paycheck before you even see it:

- **Recruiting costs.** The employer has to find you and get your attention. This happens online, at career events, or by putting a sign in the window. Every position needs to be filled, all the way to high-level recruitment for senior positions. Costly, to say the least.
- **Training.** The materials you'll need to get started cost

money. Things like computers, software, uniforms, desks, stupid potted plants, and that ergonomic mouse pad that you didn't ask for with the weird hump by your wrist—all that's coming out of your salary. You're welcome! Plus, they usually have to pay another staff member to train you and get you up to speed, or at least pay someone else to do the job you should be doing while you're still getting trained.

- **Health insurance**—if you're working full-time (forty hours per week). This is why many minimum-wage employers will let you work only 38.5 hours per week, which can make it hard to pull yourself up by your bootstraps. But that is a whole 'nother discussion! Point is, insurance is costing you, and it's probably more expensive to get it from your employer than it would be to purchase your own.
- **Financial programs.** Some companies offer 401(k) matching programs, stock options, and other financial incentives, which are great. But they will also cut into your salary in many cases.
- **Overhead.** This includes any physical office space and all the utilities and other recurring costs that come with the building the employer occupies.
- **Management and executive salaries.** Yeah . . . often quite disproportionate.

The list goes on and on! By the time your salary is up for discussion, it's less about what you're worth and more what they can afford. In some cases, a job that deserves one hundred thousand dollars is getting fifty thousand or less!

Can you negotiate your salary? Absolutely. But even at the highest level of negotiation, it's very unlikely that you're going to make as much money within a company as you'll make taking that exact same expertise and applying it outside of the company for your own gain. The skills you acquire along your journey are yours to use as you wish, at a price that you command. Now you just need to identify which of your on-the-job skills is ripe for the picking, start developing your idea, and then find your customers. (Don't worry, I'll fill in the how-tos as we continue.)

3. **Things people ask you for.** Besides the seemingly interminable amount of time spent in school, I think one of the biggest turnoffs for me about a career in medicine would be the relentless questions from well-intentioned civilians looking to "pick my brain" off the clock about a medical problem they are having, rather than setting up an appointment to have it properly examined by a physician with expertise in that area.

"Do you have a quick second? I wanted to get your opinion on this lump in my neck." "I've been having this weird pain in my chest. It's a bit like indigestion, but it's a little bit sharper. I always get it after I eat spicy foods. Any idea what that could be?" On and on these questions would go. But that's how it goes with many professions. For example, if you have a friend who is an attorney, you might find yourself shooting him a text that says something like, "Can you go to jail for unpaid parking tickets . . . hypothetically?"

We do the same thing when it comes to personal matters too. If you have a friend who's always getting dumped and you just broke up with your boyfriend of five years over some steamy texts between him and that bimbo at work who you knew he had a crush on, you'd know exactly which friend to call and vent to about that douche bag, wouldn't you?

The point here is that whether you realize it or not, we lean on experts to help us figure things out—and if people keep asking you for help, advice, or insight in a particular area, there's a good chance that others look at you as the expert or "go-to" in their circle of influence.

You have to start paying more attention to things that people ask you for. If someone asks you to help them with something, your mind should immediately begin assessing whether this is something that could become profitable.

Let that subliminal capitalistic brain fire up! Do you have friends who are always asking you for diet advice? What about people who are constantly asking for your insights into their relationships? Do friends and family call you to watch their dogs when they go out of town? Start paying attention to the things that people require of you; then eventually, you'll get paid to do things that you used to do for free.

My girlfriend's brother, Caleb, started a moving company because he was tired of people asking him to move their junk for free. He bought one of those Ford F-350s, and people started coming out of the woodwork: *"Can you help me move my ten-thousand-volume book collection?"* *"I'm moving on Sunday. Think I could 'borrow' your truck?"*

Caleb is a nice guy, so typically he said yes. They were his friends, after all. Until one day, he had an idea . . .

> **Friend:** *"Caleb, I need someone to help me move this three-thousand-pound sectional couch. Can you come over with your truck and help this weekend?"*

Caleb: *"Sure, my rate is sixty dollars an hour."*
Friend: *"OK . . . great! See you then!"*

And just like that, a business was born. He paid attention to what the market was already asking him for and just gave the people what they wanted. He started getting more and more business, then used some of that money to buy another truck and begin expanding.

If people ask you for something, it could be worth charging for!

4. Things you want to learn. After teaching college test prep for a while, my second successful freelance business—which I also quickly scaled to over a hundred thousand dollars—was a web design company called Primal Digital. And guess what? I barely knew anything about web design in the beginning!

The idea started on a whim. I'd already had a bit of success with my first business as an SAT tutor, and I was looking for something that I could do from my house. I was not an expert by any means. I knew just enough to get a basic, one-page site up on WordPress, and that was about it. It's almost embarrassing to think about as I type it now. I set up my web design company's one-page website with a very fancy theme, to give the appearance that I was much more established than I actually was, and proceeded to start posting on popular freelance job boards like Upwork (Elance/oDesk at the time) and a few others. Within a few hours, I started getting bites for $1,000, $2,000, and even $5,000 jobs! WTF?!

I'll outline some of the strategies that skyrocketed me past my peers in a bit; what I want you to focus on right now is my relative lack of knowledge about the subject area. How was I able to get away with this?

My first few clients were happy to pay me because even though I wasn't a world-class expert, I still knew more than they did about building a website. Remember, for someone who doesn't use computers much outside of Google and Facebook, even setting up a basic WordPress blog is a damn near mystical process.

I worked my way up doing simple work, and as my skill set improved, I was able to charge more and more for my services. I essentially paid myself to learn how to build websites.

You could do the same thing easily. Find a skill or idea that you're a beginner in but that you want to become really good at. Then gradually improve that skill set and find customers who are willing to pay you as you learn. It's like paying yourself to go to school for something that you actually care about. You don't have to start as an expert. It's OK if you haven't done this before. You'll get better with time—and you can get paid in the process.

How to Leverage Your Existing Job Skills

People who know Kaplan Test Prep probably recognize the name from their nightmares: They are the biggest standardized test prep organization in the United States.

If you ever had to take a big high school or college exam, there's a good chance you've been subjected to one of their grotesquely enormous purple workbooks.

Most people look at their time studying for these types of highly regulated tests as an absolute waste of time, and I can't say that I'd disagree in most cases.

But for me, taking standardized tests opened far more doors than the university alone. Truth is, I've always been a pretty good test taker. If the test was fill-in-the-bubble, I pretty much always aced it—including my SAT.

This natural inclination helped me to land a job with Kaplan in college teaching high school juniors and seniors reading and math for the SAT. At the time, I was thrilled at my wages: eighteen dollars an hour! Sometimes I'd even get twenty dollars an hour with overtime. I thought this was great because I was a poor college kid (typical), and also because I mistakenly compared the idea of a "decent" wage to minimum wage. *Minimum wage is, like, seven dollars . . . so this is almost three times the minimum wage!* (Minimum wage in the United States has been artificially depressed for decades, so using it as a barometer for how well you're doing is a SURE strategy to remain broke.)

Like I said, I was pretty happy with this pay—until I went to a student's house for a private tutoring session one day. The student was upstairs getting her materials so we could start our session, and I was at the dining room table. One of the Kaplan brochures caught my eye, and I started flipping through it and landed on the page with the hourly rates they charged tutees for sessions with each of their tutors. *They were charging the family a hundred dollars an hour for me to be there.*

I had to do a double take. I thought to myself, *So, let me get this straight . . . I'm doing all the driving to and from the houses, totaling hours of driving time every week . . . I'm doing all the teaching and grading of the tests—often by hand, if Kaplan's machines are broken . . . I'm doing all the communication with the students and the parents . . . I'm the only one who has actually taken an SAT test in the recent past and can relate to the experience . . . and yet Kaplan is taking 82 percent of every dollar that I make?*

Ridiculous.

I was upset, but at that point in my life I didn't really know what to do, so I had to "suck it up" and keep working for eighteen dollars an hour. However, years later when I remembered this story, teaching the SAT was my go-to. I launched my test prep business and scaled it to more than a hundred thousand dollars in a matter of months.

Bottom line: Leveraging your existing on-the-job skills can really pay off.

The Possibilities Are Endless

The great thing about freelancing is that it creates so many opportunities for you to try your hand at different ideas, quickly validate whether the idea is good, and then decide to ramp it up (or scale back) if you choose. Just looking into the four main "buckets" listed earlier and then qualifying those ideas using the Three-Question Validation technique, my students have launched businesses in hundreds of fields, all over the world—some a bit more unconventional than you might expect:

- Personal trainers. (Getting in shape is everyone's number one priority. Every year.)
- Artists and musicians. (I learned guitar from a freelance guitar instructor. I paid him in real money.)
- Athletes. (If you excel at a sport, you need to be teaching someone and getting paid for it.)
- Pastry chefs and caterers. (Yum!)
- Tutors (elementary, middle, high school).
- Marketers (funnels, landing pages, automation, etc.).
- Web developers and designers. (WordPress skills alone are HUGE!)
- Accountants and bookkeepers. (They are a MUST for small businesses.)
- Writers and authors. (Copywriting, specifically, is a great skill to have!)
- Nutrition coaches. (One of my students, Daniel, has his clients submit pictures of what they just ate so that he can give them feedback on food quality and portion sizes!)
- Yoga teachers (especially if you live in an area that's "trendy").
- Pet sitters and dog walkers. (Busy moms and executives can't be home during the day to let Rover out. But you can.)
- Consultants. (Small biz consulting is huge, but if you have a very specialized area of expertise, the sky is the limit.)

- Interior decorators and personal shoppers. (They get paid to show people how to make their house and/or body look amazing.)
- Personal assistants (also known as "gophers").
- Magicians and entertainers. (They make kids cry at parties.)
- Event planners. (They plan parties where kids will hopefully cry.)

And this list is nowhere near exhaustive. Just find the intersection of what you like and what you're good at and you're likely to find a market.

A few years back, Deloitte (a huge corporate consulting firm) did a survey that showed 44 percent of millennials expected to leave their employer within the next two years. The main reason: lack of career progression. Sound familiar?

The U.S. Bureau of Labor Statistics and U.S. Census shows a crazy increase in the amount of self-employed, freelance, and independent contractors over the last few decades, up from 17 percent of the workforce in 1989 to a projected 43 percent by 2020. What do you think will happen by 2030? Are you paying attention? #Gigantopithecus.

Growth in Contingent Workforce

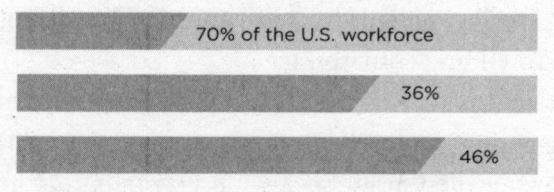

70% of the U.S. workforce

36%

46%

U.S. Bureau of Labor Statistics and U.S. Census

Thinking Right Next to the Box

What if after reading all these strategies, you still can't think of an idea that you'd be good at?

That's a pretty common problem, believe it or not.

First, remember this: You don't have to build your entire business overnight. You don't even have to build it tomorrow, or this week.

One of the pitfalls of reading how-to or self-help books is that they often don't indicate a time frame for you to help yourself. You start reading all the success stories, and naturally, you want to see results in your own life as quickly as possible.

I get it. And I want you to be successful quickly as well. But don't pressure yourself to do everything at once.

If you read this entire chapter and you still can't come up with a good idea to try, continue to go through it again and try tomorrow. Then the next day. Nine times out of ten, the problem isn't that you can't think of a good idea; the problem is usually that you've thought of several ideas but immediately discarded them because your internal monologue said, *That won't work. Don't even try!*

Don't fall for this. Run the ideas through Three-Question Validation. Start looking for clients who will pay you for your services (we'll cover this in depth shortly). Test things. Break things. You'll find something.

It all begins with TESTING. If you test several ideas and nothing really "catches on," sometimes it's appropriate to reposition your offer or niche down even more. In many cases, the idea you're looking for is right around the corner, within arm's reach. In fact, my friend and mentor Stephen Key, best-selling author of the book *One Simple Idea* and a prolific inventor in his own right, has a better way to describe this process. He calls it "thinking right next to the box" as opposed to "thinking outside of the box."

For instance, perhaps you want to leverage your skills as a personal trainer but can't think of an idea that's unique enough to stand out. Rather than think about *what* you want to do, think about *who* you want to serve and the *specific result* they'll achieve by working with you. It usually helps if this group of people has an obvious need that fits in with your offer.

For example:

"I'm a personal trainer . . ."
Becomes: *"I help busy moms lose their first fifteen pounds and look great naked."*

"I'm a piano instructor . . ."
Becomes: *"I teach first-time musicians how to play their favorite song on the piano in four weeks or less."*

"I'm an app designer . . ."
Becomes: *"I'm a UX/UI specialist who focuses on tech start-ups making five hundred thousand to one million dollars a year."*

The answer was right in front of your face the entire time. You didn't have to search the entire universe to find it. All you had to do was look right next to the box and make a small, meaningful adjustment to your approach.

How to Find Clients Who Want to Pay You Big Money for Your Work

One of the biggest challenges at the beginning of your journey will be, without a doubt, finding customers, clients, and other people who appreciate what you do so much that they're willing to give you money in exchange for it.

But then again, this is the purpose of a business, isn't it? Lots of people love the idea of becoming an entrepreneur. They embrace the cute memes on Instagram about "hustle" and "grind," but when push comes to shove, they never do the single most important thing for all businesses; SELL SHIT!

Without any experience, it will probably be pretty nerve-wracking to ask potential customers (often strangers, at that) to buy from you.

But here's the good news: You don't have to start from scratch. The customers are out there, ready and waiting to throw their money at you. Now it's your job to find them. Once you find them, convincing them to buy isn't nearly as hard as you think.

The Marsupial Method is an intelligent, ultrafast networking strategy that I developed to help me get a jump-start finding customers when I had literally zero connections.

So let's find 'em :)

The Marsupial Method

The most popular example, and the one most people think of when they hear the word *marsupial*, is the kangaroo. But there are many different types of these animals. If you google "list of marsupials," be prepared to be overwhelmed with warm tinglies. They're freaking adorable. (Whatever you do, DO NOT type in "baby wallaby." Just trust me on that.)

One of their most interesting characteristics is that since they give birth to live but relatively underdeveloped offspring, all female marsupials have a small pouch on the outside of the body. It functions as a second, external womb. When the baby (called a *joey*) is born, it crawls from the first womb to the pouch, where it continues to develop. Usually the mother's nipples are actually inside the pouch!

In some cases, the mother even allows the joey to leave and reenter the pouch well after it can fend for itself. Why? The pocket offers food, protection, and stability—an ideal place to grow.

Just like the joey, you can find other, more established business owners who are willing to share their resources—particularly their clients—with you to help you build your business under their protection. It takes relatively little work on your part to set up this type of arrangement, and the dividends will pay off almost immediately—sometimes the same day. That's how quickly the Marsupial Method can help you find paying customers.

Then, when you get big enough to find your own clients and you have a steady stream of people knocking on your door, you can still use these valuable relationships to boost your bottom line. It's an incredibly powerful weapon.

The Four-Part Marsupial Method Framework

There are four essential steps to making the Marsupial Method work for you:

- **Step 1:** Identify who your customers are. Are they single dads, stay-at-home moms, or active families of four? Hint: Do your research. Don't just assume you know who your target market is. They may not be the most obvious people. As a general rule, they should be people who have money and decision-making authority.

- **Step 2:** Identify which businesses those customers are ALREADY working with. Look for businesses that share your target customer base and, if possible, have services that complement yours or are related without directly competing. For instance, if you're a nutritionist who wants to find clients, the local health food store would be a good place to look.

- **Step 3:** Offer the existing business and their customers MASSIVE value. Going back to the health food store example, they will no doubt have a stream of clients who are interested in losing weight. After all, they're selling healthy food. If that store directed their customers to you (perhaps in a flyer or email) and you got new clients for your nutrition coaching as a result, you pay them a percentage of your profit and then set up your clients' meal plans in such a way that they have to return to the health food store to buy most or all of the items! This is the ultimate win-win-win scenario for all parties involved!

- **Step 4:** Collect the stream of leads and customers by "staying in the pocket" like a marsupial. Over time, as you work with more and more partners, this process will generate more and more referral business for you through word of mouth. It's an endless cycle, and everybody is getting the "good end" of the deal.

To state the method simply: Find a business that has the same type of customer you want to attract. Then, find a service or product you can offer that complements what the other business is providing without competing or stepping on their toes. Offer to provide that service to the other business's clients (perhaps with a special rate) and then pay them a percentage of the money you make from working with their clients.

Remember: The real key to making the Marsupial Method work is finding other, more established businesses to team up with, and then creating win-win-win scenarios that add value to their business, their customers, and yourself. If you can make them a ton of money in the process, that helps too.

Now, I'll tell you how I used this strategy to launch my tutoring business and scale it up to a hundred thousand dollars in less than a year.

I WAS IN ATLANTA at the time, and I was BEYOND ready to leave the restaurant. Thinking back to my experience working at Kaplan (and using the Three-Question Validation technique, of course), I knew that opening up a test prep business would be profitable.

The idea was there; now I just needed to find people who

wanted to pay me to teach them. The first thing I did was start looking for other private tutors online, to scope them out and get some intel. *That's step 1 of the Marsupial Method.*

Specifically, I was looking to find out:

- What rates they were charging per hour
- What types of classes they were offering
- What types of material they were using to teach

I was looking for any information that could give me a clue as to how I was supposed to find clients, because I had no idea. Was I supposed to put an ad on Craigslist and pray? Run a help wanted ad in my local newspaper? Or maybe I should have posted one of those annoying "take one" fliers on the community bulletin board, with a few dangling chads already removed, as if to indicate that other people were calling left and right!

It all just seemed terribly inefficient.

I doubted my competition was making any money using these slow, outdated, overcrowded methods; plus, I didn't really think my target market—mainly high schoolers and their parents—would be looking in these places for SAT help. So where would they be looking instead?

At this point, I drew a bit on my experience teaching the test a few years earlier. High schools generally don't teach standardized test preparation in the curriculum. It's kind of absurd, considering that a huge part of the college admissions process is based on standardized test scores. But that's the truth. Take it up with your local councilman.

Instead, schools usually recommend one of the "big-box"

prep companies (Kaplan, Princeton Review, etc.) to families. This is essentially a "one size hopefully fits most" approach. Unfortunately, the schools usually aren't able to do a very thorough assessment of whether sessions with these third-party test prep companies are even working—or whether they are the best value for families.

On the other side of the fence, most parents are so overwhelmed by all the testing and college talk that they generally defer to the school and the guidance counselors when it comes to test prep. Whoever the school recommends, parents usually hire. In cases where the school doesn't have a preferred service provider, parents usually just ask around and find out where the parents of older students sent their kids the year before.

It's the blind leading the blind! Seems it would be hard to edge my way in as an independent service provider, eh?

I was trying to figure out a way to break through the noise when I stumbled across something interesting in my research: In Atlanta (and all over the country, I'd later find out) there's a small group of elite "admissions coaches" that work with private schools to prep kids for applying to ivy-league schools. These coaches are intense, often "grooming" children for five to ten years to be top candidates. *Identifying these private consultants was step 2.*

No stone was left unturned: From academics to extracurriculars, admissions essays, and help with their applications, these private coaches knew how to churn out world-class applicants. Of course, they also advised students and families on where to go for the best standardized test prep. The coaches held a great deal of influence.

A few things stood out to me almost immediately:

- These coaches worked directly with the parents—who, let's face it, were the real customers here.
- Yes, I'd be teaching the students, but all the business would be handled between "adults." The parents were the ones with the money and the decision-making power. If we were going to do any business at all, they were going to have to like me and trust me. I had to impress them first. (Hint: Know who your real customer is!)
- Since most times these admissions coaches didn't actually teach test prep, they simply referred the parents to work with Kaplan or Princeton Review to get the kid ready for the test.

I saw my opportunity. I offered to step in and handle this problem for the coaches. My logic: They were losing money because they didn't have the skill set to teach or the bandwidth to handle many students at once. Luckily for me, I had the skill set and all the time in the world. If I could just get in front of them and convince them to let me be their go-to referral source for test prep, I would have more work than I knew what to do with—literally overnight.

Think about it like this: You have a skill set. There are existing businesses that have audiences, customers, and clients who need that skill set. What can you do to make these existing businesses want to work with you so badly that it's a no-brainer? The number one thing you provide them is most likely a financial incentive.

I approached these consultants with an offer they couldn't refuse.

Here was the basic pitch: They would refer their clients to me, and they got to "white label" my service. That meant they essentially brought me in-house as a member of their team, even though I remained independent. *That's step 3 of the Marsupial Method.*

Why would they do this? The arrangement offered two major payoffs:

Major Payoff 1: Having an in-house test prep service added to the perceived value of their company and impressed their clients. It's always nice to have a one-stop shop. Parents are busy enough; this just made their lives easier.

Major Payoff 2: I agreed to do a fifty-fifty revenue split with them on any large classes I taught (ten-plus students) and a seventy-thirty split on any one-on-one students—particularly when I had to drive to the student's house.

For them, this was found money that they would have never had access to previously. Do you think Kaplan and Princeton Review were cutting them checks for the referrals? I think not!

On the other hand, I got the instant hookup with clients I would have never otherwise met. The admissions coaches literally had a Rolodex of people they could call and introduce me to within a few days. (Rolodex? Google it.)

But the deal got even sweeter: Because I was getting so many new clients at once, I could afford to be significantly cheaper than the competing test prep services. In many cases, I cut my rates in half compared to the big-box stores and still made incredible money: from $80 to as much as $150 an hour in some cases.

That's what I call "doctor money."

An important point: I didn't see my revenue sharing with these consultants as merely "cutting them a check." I saw it as paying for access to their large network of clients and associates. I did this—as corny as it may sound—gratefully. There is a certain amount of danger that you'll work with a partner and eventually wonder, *What are they doing for me? I'm doing all the work*. On the front end, that may be true. But the sheer number of referrals you'll get as a result of using this method over an extended period of time will most likely outweigh the initial "cost" of having to share some money with them. Any word-of-mouth referral you get as a result of your work doesn't have to be part of the revenue-split deal, and you can always renegotiate your deal later if you're no longer feeling comfortable.

Parents were happy because they were saving a ton. Consultants were happy because I was making them thousands of dollars and filling their offices with happy parents. I was happy because I was able to get the hell out of LongHorn Steakhouse. *(Naturally, that's step 4!)*

Using the Marsupial Method via "Cold" Email

You can expand your reach with the Marsupial Method by using email to find and contact other potential partners. But the process of approaching other, more successful businesses can be harrowing to beginners. There's nothing more uncomfortable than cold-calling someone you don't know.

If you know what you're doing, you can learn how to quickly create concise, persuasive emails that even busy people will respond to. The key to successful cold emails is getting the decision-makers to open your emails and take action.

How to Write a Great Cold Email

The central focus of any cold email should be to offer lots of value to the other person and show them why working with you is a no-brainer.

In the example below, I'm a web designer and the other business owner is a social media consultant. I'm contacting the consultant because I see a potential partnership opportunity that could make us both a lot of money.

Keep in mind that this is just a template. Feel free to use the framework, but make it your own too. Adjust the offer to your industry, use your own language, and inject your own personality. (To help you understand the purpose of each part of the email, I've added explanations in [brackets] below.)

Subject: Teaming up to offer your customers an even better experience

[The best subject lines state what the email is about succinctly and clearly. No need to be cute.]

Hi Mr. Smith,

My name is Daniel, and I run a web development company called XYZ. [Get right to the point.]

I see that you work in social media consulting [insert related field]. *That's really cool/interesting/exciting. It looks like you're doing great work with XYZ project.* [Show that you did your research.]

I'm sure you have many clients who need an awesome website to match all the great work you're doing with them on social media.

I would love to be the "go-to" when your clients need help! I have a few ideas that might make us both a lot of money and make our clients really happy as well [benefit driven].

May I send you a sixty-second breakdown via email? [Make it easy for them. All they have to say is yes.]

Thanks and looking forward to hearing from you,

Daniel

That's an extremely basic and relatively dry approach, but it communicates all the key elements.

One question that you might be thinking: Why bother to send an additional email with details when I could have just explained everything in one email? The reasons for this are equal parts business etiquette and sneaky persuasive psychology. Since most people are naturally guarded, it's going to be hard to find other businesses that are willing to partner with you just because you showed up in their in-box and pitched them on the spot. Asking for permission to send them your *extremely brief* idea turns the interaction from outbound marketing (where you approach them and pitch without their consent) to inbound marketing (where they request information from you in order to learn more). It's a simple shift, yet very powerful.

Once you get a yes, follow up on your initial email with a quick email explaining the partnership. If they like it, get on the phone and close the deal.

To be clear, this isn't a magical formula. Most people will still have reasons they don't want to partner up with you, and that's totally fine. You don't need everybody. All you need are a few really good partners to bring you a steady stream of clients. So keep trying! Persist!

Using "Warm Canvassing" and Establishing Expert Positioning

Sometimes partnering with other businesses isn't the best solution. Sometimes you just need to find your customers and pitch them on your services directly. It'll take some guts, some negotiation skills, and a keen understanding of why people buy things in the first place.

The Warm Canvassing Method

Looking back on it, it's almost comical how my school would thrust a new holiday cookie sale on us every three months.

Preying on soft parents with their children's smiles. Forcing them to buy steel tins of dry, sugary treats every Thanksgiving and Christmas.

It was always stressful for me as well. I don't know about you, but I always HATED doing school fund-raisers. I was never motivated by the prizes they gave out for selling the most, and the process of walking door-to-door pitching cookies is terrifying for a ten-year-old.

Years later, in college, I got a summer job working as an environmental activist, going door-to-door collecting donations. This is called "cold canvassing." It wasn't my first choice, but I needed money!

The catch: My salary was entirely based on commission. The more money I got in donations, the bigger my paycheck. Sounded great at the time. But looking back now, it was a horrible idea. They stuffed me and four other starving students into a van, dropped us in a sweltering Florida suburb with a stack of clipboards, and said, "OK, champ! Go do your thing!"

A few hours later, when I hadn't even mustered up the courage to knock on a single door, one of their "trainers" came to give me some pointers. Somewhere after her exaggerated demonstration of how to smile and right before her explanation of why eye contact and handshakes are important, I dipped out. Cold canvassing and door-to-door sales were never my thing. I don't like pitching random people my services. It makes me uncomfortable!

But if the other people and I already have a relationship, talking to them is a breeze. This realization helped me develop the concept of warm canvassing.

How It Works

Warm canvassing is simple on the surface: Find your ideal customers in their "natural habitat," the place where they are most likely to be interested in hearing about your offer, and the place where it would be most natural to talk about your services without any weird "salesy" tension.

This scenario might present itself in several different ways, depending on what your skill set is. For instance, let's say you wanted to use warm canvassing to start finding clients for your dog-walking side business. Instead of going door-to-door hundreds of times in your neighborhood, hoping each door you knock on is a potential customer, why not laser-target the people who you know will be interested by walking around in your neighborhood and approaching people who are already out walking their dogs?

It's much more natural to approach someone who is already walking and say, "Hey, my name is Sara. I live right around the corner and walk dogs for a few other people in the neighborhood on the side. If you ever need anybody, here's my card," rather than use the "spray and pray" technique, hoping something hits.

Focus on Professionals

One way to make this process even easier is to use your existing network of friends and colleagues to carefully pick the people or businesses that might be best suited to work with you. In particular, I like to look at all the relationships I have with professionals in various fields, especially people I've patronized or worked with: doctors, lawyers, real estate agents, chiropractors, architects, some successful entrepreneurs— essentially anybody who is secure financially and is a decision-maker in a small- to medium-size company or private practice:

- Doctors need better websites, more SEO juice, and better email management. Can you help them with any of that?
- Property owners need their buildings repainted. Are you handy with a brush?
- Real estate agents need better video of the properties they are listing so that they can attract more interest and make more sales. Do you know how to shoot video?
- Lawyers need help marketing and getting exposure. Can you write compelling content and help them get an email newsletter started?

Look on Kickstarter and see which projects are taking off and getting 200 percent funding; there's a good chance the owner of that business might need some help for their upcoming launch. What help can you provide?

If you can do, make, or build something to help them, you can get them to hire you. Find these professionals in your immediate and extended network (one or two degrees of separation is fine) and start pitching them your services.

These types of people are great to work with because they typically have money and connections to other pros in their field—who are also willing to spend on promotion and overall improvement—but they're likely to be much "warmer" to your approach because you're coming to them with something that they already need. They are also prime candidates for your pitch because they typically don't know much about anything outside of their chosen field.

Getting Your Foot in the Door with "Free" Work

In a world where college is dead, I'm afraid to say the same may be true for résumés. In today's economy, with the speed of business moving faster and faster each year, the best way to stand out to your customers is not just to tell them how good you are, but to show them. Once you've identified who your target audience is using warm canvassing, I suggest using free work to get your foot in the door.

Look at it this way: Have you ever gotten mad at the supermarket for giving out free samples? Of course not! We love free.

The same concept applies when you're looking to break into a new industry or career. Let potential customers or clients sample the goods (your work) before paying. Not only will it make your pitch MUCH easier; it will leave a great impression and brings tons of referrals your way.

Making Forty Thousand Dollars in Six Hours of Free Work

At the end of 2013, after a few years of building up different hustles to over a hundred thousand dollars, I took it upon myself to advise the world on all matters business. Naturally, I became a consultant. My specialty: high-performing landing pages, emails, and sales copy. I had some serious skills; now I just had to find clients.

I knew my skills would appeal mostly to people who had online businesses, so I started asking around my network of friends to see if they knew anybody who could use my services. Within a day or so, I had my first lead. The business had a podcast worth seven figures in their résumé and an audience in the millions, so it was an incredible opportunity. They needed somebody to help them tighten up their copywriting. The pay would be excellent. But how was I supposed to prove I was the right guy for the job?

We set up a dinner meeting for three or four days later. I went to work in my Moleskine notebook analyzing their business and sketching out how I wanted the meeting to go. I knew I would have to go all-out and show them what I could do ahead of time if I was going to have a chance.

I SPENT THE NEXT FEW DAYS preparing to meet the partners at the podcast I was hoping to work with. I wrote down tons of questions in my Moleskine notebook so that I could show them that I took their work seriously and wanted to find the best way to help them.

Here's what I jotted down:

Preliminary Questions

- What's your current revenue like? How many email subscribers do you have, and how many are you getting per month?
- What are your biggest projects and priorities right now?
- Have you ever hired outside consultants before?
- What's the attrition rate of your membership program?

Note: These preliminary questions have two purposes:

1. To see if they actually have their shit together. Do they actually know their numbers and core issues? If not, working with them will be hard.
2. To allow me to write down their responses in my notebook and make little ad-libs like *"Hmm, interesting"* and *"Wow, OK!"* Funnily enough, the appearance of you listening to their information and evaluating it, then writing something in your book, really does create an air of authority— like a doctor diagnosing a patient. As I looked down at my notes, I'd often chuckle to myself. I couldn't help feeling a bit like Kramer playing Dr. Van Nostrand at times.

Detailed Questions

- Have you thought about how to create a "cascading" effect that ties all your products together in a logical sequence and that makes leads/customers more likely to buy more than once?
- Is there a specific reason why you haven't created funnels for all your products, especially the most lucrative ones? (For them, it was live events.)
- Do you have any insight on current segmentation? Specifically, how do you know individual reader and listener interests and if they are ready to buy without having to call them?
- Hypothetical: If you work on a campaign and it doesn't do well, what do you do? Is there a systematic map for improving it?

- Have you thought about the specific strategies you're going to use to grow (by two times, five times, or even ten
times) the business?

Note: Every single one of these more detailed questions is
designed to make the potential client see their own gap in
knowledge.

How to Get a Job at a Kick-Ass Start-Up Using Free Work

For the past year, Aaron has been helping us grow, providing
resources, encouragement, and intel to everyone in the
Rich20 community. He started off by just being super engaged with the community, leaving thoughtful comments on
posts and sharing his ideas.

I started to notice his name popping up in the newsfeed
over and over. *I wonder what this guy is up to? He seems to be a
pretty good dude,* I'd think. He definitely had my attention. So
when he offered to help out a bit more, I made him an admin
in the Facebook community. Then he turned up the heat and
started giving value in a MASSIVE way. For instance, he
went above and beyond to create an interactive map of where
all our members are located in the world. He also began at-
tending my webinars and answering questions from attend-
ees. It was getting to the point where I was so overwhelmed
with gratitude for all he was doing for us gratis that I figured
we at least needed to see if there was somewhere he might fit
in the company. So I flew him out from DC to LA and put
him up in a dope Airbnb by the beach just to learn a bit more

about him. He'd already invested in us, so we decided to invest in him as well.

One thing I should mention about Aaron: He doesn't necessarily *need* the money. He has a few successful companies in addition to many years as a professional poker player. There is no "if this, then that" ulterior motive underlying his actions. So it was clear he was helping us out because he genuinely wanted to. His hustle was so real we HAD to hire him. I literally had no choice. My team MADE me do it.

If you want to work with awesome people doing work you care about, you don't need a good résumé. You only need to genuinely help people accomplish things. (Ironically, we're now just going to PAY Aaron to do many of the things he was already doing. Pretty sweet deal.)

Free work can be a path to making a great living because it makes hiring you an absolute no-brainer. So try volunteering or contributing to a company or organization you like or want to work for, for free, and very likely you will soon find yourself raking in the big bucks.

Expert Positioning
(aka "Calling Their Baby Ugly")

One mistake beginning freelancers make is considering themselves to be at the mercy of other people and businesses when it comes to getting hired for decent rates. This is a dangerous and inaccurate pattern of thought.

Remember, this is a partnership. Yes, they are paying you money. But you also bring valuable, much-needed skills to the table. You are the expert in your discipline, and you need to make sure that your clients know this in a clear but unabrasive way.

The first step in establishing yourself as an expert is just being great at what you do (or being confident that you can find the right person for the job). But in addition to getting the job done, you also must learn the fine art of displaying your expertise.

One way to display your expertise is by asking thought-provoking questions that show you've put a great deal of consideration into your work, and that show you know how to fix the problems your potential customers are having. This style of questioning, also known as "calling their baby ugly," is designed to show your potential clients how much you know, how much value you bring to the table, and how much they could be overlooking by not working with you.

It's the equivalent of saying to someone, *"What you have right now probably won't work. But don't worry, I know how to fix it."*

Quick Recap

Whatever way you look at it, a nine-to-five isn't true independence, because you have to be somewhere from nine until five or you'll be fired. And that's where freelancing comes in. You can freelance while you're at your nine-to-five, scale it up, and then do it full-time. Working whenever you want—that's more like true independence. And this whole entrepreneurship thing just isn't as risky as the media makes it out to be. Or it's just about as risky as anything else. Remember the medical school example? The amount of dedication and perseverance and money (!) that you have to have to even qualify—and yet nobody talks about medical school as a risk. Something that will mitigate your risk of failure as an entrepreneur is Three-Question Validation: 1) Is there competition in my space? 2) Are my competitors making money? 3) Can I do my idea differently and/or better? If you can answer yes to all three questions, then you can start your business today. And one way to start your business is to use the Marsupial Method. Find those more established businesses, research where you can help them, like I did with my SAT test prep company, and you'll create a win-win-win scenario— because you'll be adding value to the more established companies, their customers, and yourself. And remember: There's nothing wrong with doing free work. If you do free work that's so good that it can't be ignored, good things will happen. Like getting hired to work for an awesome start-up company. Like Rich20Something Media Inc. Just saying.

8

Going Digital: How to Create an Online Business That Makes Money While You Sleep

If your business is not on the Internet,
then your business will be out of business.
—Bill Gates

KEY TAKEAWAYS:

$ It's entirely possible to make money while you sleep; this is the new American dream:

$ Passive income does not mean that you don't have to work hard for your money—#sorrynotsorry.

$ First was the agricultural age. Then it was the industrial age. Now it's the information age. And there are many different ways to make money online; it's not just through selling stuff on eBay.

$ Everybody can be a content consumer, and everybody can be a content creator.

$ Making money through an online business isn't magic;

> it's math. And that means you have to take care of your
> community. Even when you have only ten people on
> your email list, get to know those ten people.

IT'S TWO THIRTY in the morning, and you've woken up from your sleep to feel the bedside table vibrating ever so slightly. A notification on your phone is making a white shadow dance across the wall next to your bed. You know you should go back to sleep, but on impulse, you grab your phone and flick your groggy fingers across the touch screen.

It's a Gmail notification bubble. Normally this could wait until later—who the hell has time to respond to emails at two thirty? Then, you read the subject line of the email:

Subject: You just received $1,297

You realize this is not spam; it's real. Holy shit! You just made almost $1,300 without lifting a finger.

What would it be like to have this happen every single night? How would it change your life to know that you have a business that pays you automatically every single day, whether or not you decide to "clock in" for work that day, no matter what country you're in, for the rest of your life?

How would your life change if you had the ultimate security of knowing that you had an army of salespeople working around the clock to make you money and you didn't have to pay them a dime?

To some people, this might sound like science fiction—or worse yet, a sleazy late-night infomercial. If you're rolling your eyes all the way to the back of your head right now, I get it. Trust me, I do. I thought the same thing. Then I discovered the power of starting an online business. And I can tell you one thing: All this, and much more, is possible.

Want to learn how I created the life of my dreams (and nearly unlimited income) building online products? Of course you do. Keep reading . . .

I'LL ADMIT, the above description of online business is a bit "hypey." Full disclosure: I took it straight from one of the sales emails for my premium training on building an online business, Startup from the Bottom. But despite being a bit over the top in its approach and copywriting, for the most part it's true. Online business is where it's at.

Something strange is happening in the business world right now. Social media is expanding to dozens of different platforms, and brand-new online start-ups are growth-hacking their way to massive success. More and more people are becoming customers of new products and services. It seems like there's something to fit every need:

- Sick of going to the mall? You can order a pair of jeans and have them shipped to your house the same day.
- Tired of driving yourself to the airport? You can push a button and a car will appear out of thin air to pick you up.
- Need to learn a new skill without paying $150,000 to some university to get a degree? You can learn virtually anything from the best professors in the world from the comfort of your home.

Businesses that were unheard of even a few years ago are making BILLIONS. Shit is getting wild, folks! Can you imagine what John D. Rockefeller would think?

Yet despite the consumption of these new products and services, hardly anybody actually knows how to go from consumer to producer. In other words, we are happy to spend our money online, but we have no idea how to make money online.

That ends now.

I'm going to lay out for you exactly how I turned Rich-20Something from a simple blog with very humble beginnings to a million-dollar empire in just a few years. In the process, I'm going to expose some of the myths about passive income and help you shift your mind-set from that of a mere spectator to that of a participant in the biggest global business revolution since the industrial era.

Learning how to make money while you sleep is the new American dream. Let me show you the way.

Freelancing versus Entrepreneurship: Is There a Difference?

A few years ago, I was watching an interview with Seth Godin, who is one of my heroes in the business world. He was explaining the core differences between entrepreneurship and freelancing. I was getting heated just listening to him!

Here's how Seth explains it:

Freelancers get paid for their work. If you're a freelance copywriter, you get paid when you work. Entrepreneurs use other

*people's money to build a business bigger than themselves so
that they can get paid when they sleep.*

When I saw this interview, I was busting my ass (and
making very good money) as a freelancer, and I had always
considered myself an entrepreneur because I had an entrepreneurial mind-set. So, understandably, I was a bit upset
over the semantics.

*"He doesn't know what he's talking about! I am TOO an en-
trepreneur!"* I grumbled.

Looking back on that, I have to chuckle. The reason I was
upset was because of the value and meaning I attached to the
word *entrepreneurship.* I saw entrepreneurs as free thinkers,
people who created their own destiny and didn't just take
what the world handed to them. Not thinking of myself as an
entrepreneur when I was working so hard to make money on
my own fucked with my self-identity.

But Seth did have a point.

Look, there is a reason that I chose to put freelancing BE-
FORE online business in this book, and the answer is pretty
simple: I think freelancing is an essential step in the entrepreneurial journey. You have to learn how to find clients, talk
to them, and get them to pay you. You have to learn how to
develop skills and ideas and test them in the marketplace.
And freelancing is great, because for all intents and purposes, you can get started immediately.

I wouldn't be where I am today without freelancing, and if
we were chilling on the porch drinking a beer together, I'd
advise you to do it too. That being said, freelancing is only
halfway there. It's a necessary bridge to get you away from

your day job and into independent living. On the other side of that bridge is full-fledged entrepreneurship.

In my eyes, the main difference between freelancing (aka "self-employment") and pure entrepreneurship comes down to time. In most cases, freelancers still exchange time for money (albeit for much more money than in a traditional job). Entrepreneurs depend on systems and employees and automation that work without their direct involvement.

The key question is: *"If I take myself out of the equation, does the business still work?"*

If your business could presumably run without you— assuming you hired someone to take your place or delegate your responsibilities to a team—then you are a true entrepreneur. If you can create enough momentum in your business that you'll still make money regardless of what you do on a day-to-day basis, then you are a true entrepreneur.

This is the holy grail. This is where you want to end up. Unlike any other business medium, online business allows this type of setup. Some people might even call this "passive" income. But does making money while you sleep really equate to passive income?

The Myth of "Passive" Income

Will an online business really make you passive income?

Yes and no. A big part of the allure of building an online business is that you can make money from anywhere in the world at any given time, and the sheer thought of being able to travel while getting paid has spawned an entire industry of Instagram accounts shouting the praises of passive income.

Pictures of pedicured toes dangling in the surf with a laptop nearby are the industry standard at this point. Yes! The freedom lifestyle!

But what is passive income, really? I don't think the insta-quotes ever go into precise detail, but I can make some assumptions about what most people think. If "active" income means you have to work for your money, I'm guessing the general public believes that "passive" income means money will come to you without working. Most people take the whole "make money while you sleep" thing to mean that you're not actually working for the money while you're awake.

Umm . . . yeah. That is false.

To be clear, there are plenty of legitimate sources of passive income. When Bill Gates or Warren Buffett check their bank accounts, the deposits they see are most likely passive income. That's investment money that's building upon itself and multiplying as a result. Or when members of the British royal family check their bank accounts, the money rolling in there is passive. Their salaries are just small pieces of the interest from an enormous amount of wealth accumulated over hundreds of years. That's super-duper passive.

As an online business owner, unfortunately, you will not really make passive income—at least not in the beginning. You're still going to have to work hard for your money; it's just a different type of work. Just like anything that makes money, building an online business is a job, and you can't expect to get promoted overnight. It takes time. It's not for the lazy or unmotivated.

After several years of running an online business, I'm only now beginning to see a bit of strictly passive income rolling in. Here's the key to making money passively: It requires a shit ton of work on the front end. You'll have to push the boulder uphill before you can let it coast down the hill. When this book flies off the shelves, I will get a royalty from the publisher for every copy sold. That money will be deposited in my bank account for years after the book is completed. I suppose that's passive income. But it still took me over five years to find an agent, get a publishing deal, write the damn book, and promote it. A lot of work has to go in on the front end to make money somewhere down the line.

Online business works the same way. Generally speaking, making money passively requires three things:

- A lead-generation system that finds customers automatically
- A system that promotes your products or services and collects payments automatically
- Time and experience in the game, so that you know what works

Can you take a guess on which of these three is most important? You're going to have to devote a significant amount of time if you ever want to create an online business that truly and consistently generates money while you sleep. There's really no way around that. It just takes time, my friend.

I'm clarifying this not to discourage you but to encourage and prepare you for what's to come. If your expectations are aligned with reality, you're much more likely to stay the course. Remember this as I dive into the elements of online business: It's not a sprint; it's a marathon. One day in the future, you will wake up, check your bank account, and see a deposit for something that you did months or years earlier. It's going to feel amazing. But it may not feel entirely passive.

How the Hell Does an Online Business Actually Make Money?

I have to admit that when people ask me what I do, I'm very nonspecific. I usually say something like, *"I do stuff online."* I say that because I'm lazy and generally don't feel like explaining, *"Well . . . I make online digital courses to teach people how to master certain skills."* That usually gets me the squinty-eyed look, as if they're saying, *"Sounds cute. What's your real job?"* If I had to have that conversation with every Uber driver, I'd probably kill myself. So I tend to keep quiet.

For some reason, whenever you mention that you have an online business, people start to get confused. They often assume that you're a tech nerd, that you have a Silicon Valley–backed start-up, or that you're doing porn. The media paints all of the online world with one brush. You're either an online entrepreneur or an offline entrepreneur. There doesn't seem to be an in-between in the public's eyes.

In reality, there are a TON of ways to make money online, and for the most part, you can make money in many of the same ways online as you can anywhere else. The online world is just a different medium to sell your products, ideas, and services.

Recent studies show that the average adult spends over twenty hours online every week. That's a part-time job—you might as well get paid for it! If, as a society, we're spending that much time in the online world, we should make it our responsibility to truly understand how to make money from all that time we are investing. Starting an online business shouldn't be a mystical process anymore. You don't need to be a tech wizard, programmer, or celebrity to make it work for you. Here are seven different ways that online businesses make money.

(Note: This is not an exhaustive list—simply a collection of some of the more popular methods. No need to email me with all the ideas I didn't include. There are a lot. I just want to give you some perspective.)

Online Business Type 1: e-Commerce

Examples: Amazon, eBay, your own website

In the good old days, if you wanted to open up a clothing boutique, you'd have to find a storefront space and open up a physical brick-and-mortar location. You'd have to worry about overhead like rent, employees, and inventory. You'd have to be in a prime location to ensure that you got enough foot traffic. And you'd have to physically go to the shop every single day.

Not anymore. Nowadays, you can find or make physical products, and rather than sell them in a "real" store, you can just sell them with the click of a button. There are lots of pre-existing platforms that allow you to list your items for sale without going through the time and hassle of opening up a real storefront. This is especially useful when you're a new company and only have one or two products to sell. Selling on another company's platform is especially great once your products begin to get traction, because the rating system on websites like Amazon generate more exposure for your business. Most online retailers also have their own websites, where they sell their products directly to the consumer.

One of the downsides of selling physical products is that production and manufacturing costs tend to eat up a lot of the profit margin; plus, you'll actually have to ship the item, another logistical hurdle and expense.

Online Business Type 2: Affiliate Marketing

Example: ClickBank

Did you ever have those contests at school to see who could sell the most chocolate bars around the holidays? Every year, my school did these ridiculous fund-raisers. They equipped an army of ten-year-olds with catalogs full of chocolates, wrapping paper, and "gourmet" popcorn and set us loose upon the community. The kid with the most sales at the end of the fund-raiser got some sort of prize. I think it was usually a pizza party for his or her class. Honestly, I can't remember because I was never good at those contests. There was usually a lot of pressure from teachers and administrators to sell at least a few, so I'd just hand the catalog to my mom and she'd get a few of her coworkers to buy some.

That, in a nutshell, is affiliate marketing. Somebody else has a product. You have a list of people that you offer their product to. The more sales you make, the bigger your reward. Usually for adults, the reward is money, not a pizza party.

This is a very attractive model for beginners who want to

break into the online world, because it seems so easy. All you have to do is sell someone else's stuff, sit back, and collect. There are even platforms like ClickBank that list thousands of products with affiliate programs. You sign up for an affiliate program, you receive a special link, and whenever somebody buys the product through your special link, you get a commission (typically 50 percent).

You CAN make a lot of money doing affiliate promotions. That part is true. But what most experts leave out is that you're going to need several other elements in place to successfully run a profitable affiliate campaign. You're going to need a decent-sized email list (or enough money to send paid traffic—a whole 'nother monster); PLUS, you'll need to have a decent working knowledge of online marketing so that people actually want to buy the damn thing. And most importantly, whatever you sell has to be a great fit for the people you're pitching to. The entire process can become considerably complex, and it definitely wouldn't be my first option if I were to start a brand-new online business.

Online Business Type 3: Google AdSense, Banner Ads

Example: Buzzfeed.com

If you ever visit a massive site like Entrepreneur.com or Forbes.com, you'll most likely notice prominent banner and pop-up ads all over the site. Sometimes they are rather innocuous; sometimes they are incredibly annoying. (While writing this, I checked Forbes.com, and they're all over there. YUCK!)

Banner ads and other "native" advertising (meaning any

advertisements found embedded in a website) typically advertise for products and services that the intended customer will most likely be interested in. In more sophisticated campaigns, these ads can even "retarget" customers and use cookies to track what websites they visit, then sell them very specific products. If you've ever felt like a certain product or ad was "following" you, this is most likely what was happening. If you start a website, you can use Google ads to place advertisements in strategic places on your site. Every time the ads get clicked, you get a very small amount of money—and in some cases, even more money if the visitor ends up buying the product. This is a classic model for generating revenue from a site, and it was huge in the early 2000s, before there were billions of websites online.

Now, it's much harder to make this model work. In order to get enough click-throughs to make a difference, you'll need hundreds of thousands, if not millions, of visitors. This is hard enough for big sites like Forbes.com to achieve. As a primary revenue generator, the model is not smart. There's also a fair amount of technical know-how required for setting this up, and it'll take a bit of time to get off the ground. So unless you have a website with one million unique visitors a month or more, don't consider this. And even with that many visitors, oftentimes the ads significantly water down the customer experience. I'm not a huge fan.

Online Business Type 4: Drop-Shipping

Example: "white label" products

Drop-shipping is, in many respects, a subset of e-commerce, as it can be done via a platform like Amazon. The primary difference between drop-shipping and other models of online business is the "white label" effect.

Here's how it works: You find a product that you want to sell, something that's in demand. Then, you find a generic manufacturer who can make the product, and you brand the product as your own. Essentially, the order comes in from the customer, you send that order to the manufacturer, and they put your label on it (thus, "white label") and send it out from their factory directly to the customer, as if it's coming directly from you.

For instance, let's say I wanted to make my own brand of protein powder. There's no way I have the capital to source all my own ingredients, build a laboratory, hire staff, and manufacture the product without a significant amount of funding. Instead, I can find one of many private laboratories around the country (and the world) who are willing to ship out their protein powder as "Daniel's XTreme Protein Burst," complete with my own label. I pay the cost for the materials and shipping, then mark up the price for the customer and make the difference.

I've experimented with this model and have had some friends who've done very well with it. If you're dead set on producing a physical product, it could be a good road for you. One of the things I don't like about this model is the inherent barrier between the company (you) and the customer. Since you're not the one directly producing and shipping the product, you're essentially just a front, which means quality control is often out of your hands. Again, not the worst model in the world, but not my personal favorite.

Online Business Type 5: SaaS (Software as a Service), App Development

Examples: Uber, Facebook, Netflix, Instagram

Everybody wants to build the next Facebook. That's the running joke. Most people who think of present-day entrepreneurship think of companies like Facebook, Uber, and Netflix as the standard. They're sexy, they're mobile, and most of them have some legendary "started in a garage" story. There are so many different services being offered at the touch of a button nowadays, it's astounding. One of my favorites in Los Angeles is an app called DoorDash. All I have to do is open up the app, select something off the menu from one of hundreds of local restaurants, and food comes hot to my house in about forty-five minutes. No need for takeout. I've gained at least ten pounds since discovering this gem!

SaaS businesses and apps are the rage in Silicon Valley because they are relatively lightweight and don't require a lot of overhead to run. All they need is scale. Just prove the concept, get the users, and keep pouring dollars in to keep growing. The reality is that the competition in the marketplace is fierce! And the average customer (at least in my experience) doesn't have a ton of loyalty. They are looking for the cheapest, fastest service. If the prices on Uber are too steep for me to catch a ride, I'll go to Lyft without reservation. If DoorDash doesn't have what I want to eat, I'll go to GrubHub without a second thought. This means growth has to be constant to dominate the space you're in; it's very hard to survive with a small, niche audience.

There's also the technical aspect. If you're not a developer or if you don't have a good developer by your side, it's going to be challenging to create something that's worth taking a second look at—by either a potential customer or an investor (which you're most likely going to need).

And most of these products and services don't become profitable for quite some time, if ever. One of the best-known Silicon Valley sweethearts, Uber, only recently became profitable in the United States, after almost ten years of operation and after seeing hundreds of millions of dollars in revenue and over fifty billion dollars in venture funding. And that's just in the United States. They're losing over a hundred million dollars in China every year. The company itself isn't in grave danger of failing; this is just a dramatic example of the fact that going the venture route with software can have some very unique challenges.

If you're 100 percent certain that this road is for you, then you already have your work cut out for you. Be my guest. But personally, it sounds like a massive pain in the ass.

Online Business Type 6: Content Partnerships

Examples: YouTube, podcasts, etc.

There was a time when you had to get signed by a major record label or production studio to get your content heard; these guys were the only ones handing out the big checks. Now, the model is completely flipped on its head.

If you do something creative, you can build an audience on a platform like YouTube and get paid to produce YouTube videos if enough people begin to watch. If you watch as much YouTube as I do, you probably hate the advertisements before the video (*Come on, come on . . . just start already*). The creators of those videos are getting paid to run those ads. There are so many different channels online, with hundreds of thousands, even millions, of viewers, which makes this type of business possible.

Everything from fitness to beauty, to cooking, to comedy—if you can make great content that people want to watch and share, you can get paid quite well. The top YouTubers are making hundreds of thousands, sometimes millions, of dollars simply from their ad partnerships with YouTube. Oftentimes, many other endorsement deals and opportunities come as a result of this exposure. It's a pretty sweet deal.

In a similar respect (though not to the same extent), you can do the same thing with podcasts. If you can create a podcast with a raving fan base and hundreds of thousands or even millions of downloads every month, advertisers will be knocking down your door to get in front of your audience. And it makes sense: You're essentially an independent, hyper-targeted radio station.

There aren't that many cons to this business model, except the fact that, as with building an app, it's hard to survive with a niche audience. Since you're making money for the amount of views, subscribers, and listens you get, it's going to be very hard to make a significant amount of money until you have a considerable amount of traffic—typically at least a hundred thousand subscribers/viewers. That's a LOT of potential customers, and in my opinion, if I have the eyes and ears of a hundred thousand people, I want to be able to market and sell to them directly. With a platform like YouTube or iTunes, you can't reach out and contact your audience directly in their in-box in order to sell to them, so you'll have to work doubly hard to build both the content platform AND the email list.

If you really want to make YouTube videos or run a killer podcast, that's great. You should do it—and they are incredible tools to blow up your brand. But if you dropped me down in the desert with nothing but a laptop and told me to make money, it wouldn't be my first move. It takes too long to build momentum, and the ROI (return on investment) doesn't really start to increase until you're far down the road.

I CAN ALREADY TELL what you're thinking: *So basically what you're saying is, all online business is difficult to start and hard to make money from?*

Ha! I've spent a few pages ripping six online business models to shreds. But that's because I've saved the best for last. I honestly believe that creating digital information products is the absolute best way to get started in online business—especially for a beginner. And online business type 7 explains why.

Online Business Type 7: Digital Information Products

Examples: Freelance Domination 2.0, Startup from the Bottom, and other Rich20Something courses

First there was the agricultural age. You can guess how people survived and made their living in that era. Then came the industrial age. Now we're in the information age. Unlike in years past, the most valued commodity in our era isn't a particular import or raw material; it's knowledge. I think the reason is fairly obvious: Information travels faster than ever nowadays.

The smartphone in your pocket is a perfect example. Who could have envisioned that we'd have a device that would literally contain the sum of human knowledge, the weather, and the final score of last night's Yankees game in the palm of our hand?

We want to be able to learn more about our world quickly, unimpeded by traditional mediums. And we don't want to have to attend a university to learn a new skill or idea. We want autonomy over our own education. A simple example is YouTube. How many times have you caught yourself using that platform as a mini trade school, searching for different how-tos in order to solve a small but pressing problem? I know that I've looked up everything from how to change a timing belt on my car, to how to correctly slice an avocado. This is simple knowledge that would have been transmitted directly from one person to another before, but that can now be learned in a fraction of the time by just entering a few search terms.

Of course, it goes deeper than cars and fruits. The information industry at large has literally ballooned over the past decade into a multibillion-dollar space that everyone seems to be getting a piece of. Online universities like Udemy and Coursera teach vital skills like design, marketing, and psychology for a fraction of the price that you'd pay a university, and you can build your own course load à la carte. Specialized platforms like Treehouse, which specializes in web development, focus on teaching just one skill set deeply and taking a beginning student from amateur to professional for a nominal monthly fee. Many Ivy League universities, like Harvard and MIT, have released a portion of their curriculum online for free, completely breaking down the barrier to higher education.

If you want to learn a skill to improve your life, the information is out there and within reach of the average consumer. All you have to do is put in the hours.

So where does this leave us as entrepreneurs?

The beauty about the info boom is that everybody can be not only a content consumer but also a content creator. Information products and digital courses are all about teaching somebody how to do something that they couldn't do before. And all of us have something unique that we can teach others. If you can learn how to package that knowledge and direct people to it, you can help the world by providing people with valuable skills—and you can help yourself by making money from what you already know.

Look, the other six online business models I listed could make you a millionaire. There's no denying it. But there are several things that are uniquely different about digital information products that make them ideal for a first (or second, or third) business:

- The learning curve tends to be a bit lower than with other business models, because you're essentially working with what you already know.
- There isn't too much confusing tech to work with: If you can check your email, you can handle 99 percent of the software required to grow an info product business.

- Info products require almost zero start-up capital, and the risk is very low. You'll have to buy a domain name and a few other things to get started, but you won't need to go looking for investors.
- The ROI is crazy. Since you don't have to worry about overhead or inventory, the majority of the money you make will be pure profit.
- You can easily automate the systems so that your products sell 24-7 without you even being there, which opens up the possibility for the "work from the beach" thing, if you desire.
- Scale is much easier with info products. In many cases, you acquire your customers at zero cost through free content, so your growth potential is virtually unlimited.

The BIGGEST benefit of this business model is the ability to completely dominate in a niche market. While many other types of businesses revolve around large traffic numbers or third-party middlemen to sell for you, you can build a successful six- or seven-figure info product empire with a very small list of customers who are highly targeted and really care about your work. If you knew how many basic, seemingly unpopular blogs were making a hundred thousand dollars a year or more, you'd be astonished!

I could go on and on about the benefits of info products, and yes, it's obvious I'm biased because I've had a lot of success in this market. But let's go a little bit deeper so that you can see exactly what type of potential you could have with a very simple product.

How Information Products Work

There are tons of different information product businesses with slightly different models, but they all revolve around the same basic format to find new customers and make sales.

Content ☛ Opt-In ☛ Email Marketing ☛ Sales Page ☛ Sale

Content: You'll start by creating something that people want to consume, typically for free. This could be written content (like a blog), audio content (like a podcast), or video content (like a YouTube channel). The idea here is to find people who are interested in what you want to talk about, and get them engaged in your conversation, so they, ultimately, decide that they want to hear from you on a regular basis. This decision is called an opt-in.

Opt-in: Once you've provided some awesome content, it's time to take the relationship to the next level by getting people to sign up for your email list. If you receive a bunch of email newsletters like I do, you've opted in to other people's content before. It's free to do so, and the idea behind this is that by giving your email address, you'll receive even more content, ideas, and updates in an area that interests you. Oftentimes, there will be an opt-in "bribe" that is given away to increase the likelihood of your signing up for the newsletter. If you want to check out a quick example, go to Rich-20Something.com and check out the opt-in bribe on my homepage.

Email Marketing: Once you have the potential customer's email address, you can start marketing to them. But savvy email marketers don't usually start with a pitch immediately. The key is giving even better free content than before— showing the reader how good your material is—and then, when the time is right, offering them a product that will interest them based on what they've read so far.

Sales Page and Sale: After a certain amount of time (it varies from business to business), you'll offer that email subscriber one of your products. Prices vary depending on the market and the type and quality of the product. There are super-low-end info products, like e-books, that cost ten to a hundred dollars. There are minicourses that can range anywhere from a hundred to a few hundred dollars. And there are big-ticket items that can cost in the thousands. Courses can use written material, videos, slideshows, and audio to communicate information. Typically you'll record all the information and put it somewhere where the customer can access it at any time. We'll cover the specifics of this process later in the chapter.

You can also use your email list to sell private coaching on a specific topic or even sell live events. The possibilities are bounded only by your imagination.

The Shocking Reality of Scale (aka "How Much Money Can I Make?")

I think the number one thing that surprises most people about info products is how much money they can make with a relatively small email list and halfway-decent marketing.

Here's a quick example: Let's say you're a bomb-ass photographer who wants to teach beginners how to get started in the industry. You decide to create a relatively inexpensive minicourse that will teach step-by-step instructions for taking great wedding photos and booking your first job. Simple enough, right?

You set up a blog and start writing about your photography ideas, and slowly, people start signing up for your email list. It doesn't happen overnight, but as the months roll by and you keep writing, the subscribers trickle in. After six months, you have your first thousand subscribers.

You make the course and price it at two hundred dollars, then promote it to your list.

The reality of any sales situation (not just online sales) is that only a fraction of people will end up being buyers. And that's OK. You don't need everyone to buy; you only want people who are engaged and interested.

Assume that of the thousand people on your list, you get a conversion rate of 5 percent, which is not unrealistic for a small, engaged list:

5% of 1,000 = 50 sales
50 sales at $200 = $10,000

That's ten thousand dollars from a small email list, after sending out just a few emails! I don't know about you, but that's a LOT of money to me. It's more than most people make in several months, and you've done it all automatically from your laptop. You didn't need a lot of customers, and there's not a ton of support needed to keep them happy.

But let's play with the numbers a bit.

Perhaps you want to turn your course into premium, all-inclusive flagship training in the photography business. It will have everything from how to turn the camera on, to how to become a full-time photographer making six figures. A program of this depth is going to require a lot more time on your part, and it's going to offer a lot more value to the customer, so you're going to charge more.

This course is going to be priced at two thousand dollars (with an option for payment plans to make it easier on people). Assume that since the price is much higher, the conversion rate is going to go down from a healthy 5 percent to 1 percent, which is the industry standard for a course of this price. Look at what happens:

1% of 1,000 = 10 sales
10 sales at $2,000 = $20,000

After tweaking your prices, even with drastically reduced conversion, you've still doubled your money. Twenty thousand dollars is a significant fraction of most people's yearly income—and you've managed to make that by simply creating a product that people need and finding ten customers somewhere in the world who are willing to pay for that value.

As your email list grows from one thousand to ten thousand to a hundred thousand, so will your profits. But it's all based on the same basic model of giving value up front for free with content, directing people to your email list, and offering them new, paid content.

It's not magic; it's just math.

Imagine that you took the same photography product and made it into a recurring product where new content was continually added and users paid fifty dollars per month to access it—similar to the Netflix model. Now, assume that your email list continues to grow and you're able to continually get people to buy this product. Some people will drop off and more will sign up as the year progresses since it's a monthly payment, but your average retention rate is about six months. Since the barrier to entry is considerably lower at fifty dollars per month, let's assume that you can keep a hundred people in the membership program at any given time.

Here's what those numbers look like for the year:

100 people × $50/month = $5,000 per month
$5,000/month × 12 months = $60,000 per year

Do you see what just happened there? By creating a fifty-dollar product, you've just made a NICE yearly salary with only one hundred people. Imagine if you got two hundred people! This is why creating information products is so powerful: It allows you to scale your knowledge and make incredible amounts of money with a small handful of customers in very small niches. This is a POWERFUL business model. (As I write this, I'm also beginning to realize why some pas-

tors are driving Bentleys. If every member of the congrega-
tion gives twenty dollars per week . . .)

Note: I'm purposely simplifying the math here so that you
can understand the opportunity at hand and the general process for creating an information product business. This isn't
some late-night infomercial where you just set it and forget
it—at least not in the beginning. It's going to take a lot of
hard work to get everything set up—but this will be the case
for any business. Hell, it's hard to clock into work every day
and work for someone else, isn't it? If you're going to be working on something, doesn't it make sense to create something
with this type of flexibility and unlimited potential?

The Secret to Standing Out in a Cluttered Online Market

My biggest fear with starting an online business was that my
work would end up obscured in some distant corner of the
Internet, collecting dust and dying a slow, painful death.
And I was right to be afraid. That's not an unreasonable fear.
There are a LOT of other websites out there. More than ever
before. There isn't one single niche that isn't saturated.
Health and fitness, beauty, money, relationships—every category of human need has been addressed. You'll probably
never create a piece of truly "new" content.

And you know what? That's OK.

So the first question to ask is, why you? Why would people
be willing to visit your site, listen to your advice, or buy your
products when there are so many other businesses out there
doing the same thing? The answer is community.

I learned this early on, but only now am I realizing how true it actually is. You have to create a community around your work and a space for people to improve themselves that is about more than you selling to them. More so than with any other business model, building a business around digital products requires you to create an environment that people want to return to often. As the owner of the digital business, you have to treat it like a physical storefront and welcome people to your humble little shop, even before you have merchandise to sell.

Remember the show *Cheers*? No? I don't really remember it either; I've just watched the reruns on late TV. But the main lines from the theme song are something that everybody is familiar with:

You wanna be where you can see our troubles are all the same.
You wanna be where everybody knows your name.

At a core level, we crave togetherness. We need a place where we can feel understood—like somebody "gets" us. When we can find that place, not only will we frequent it, but we'll bring our friends to it. That's how a community is grown: person by person, one at a time, until everybody there is somebody you'd love to sit and have a beer with. In the digital world, this translates to interaction and engagement. You have to be present.

I did this aggressively in the early days of Rich20 to build my community. I would respond to every comment on my blog, often asking a follow-up question to incite more thoughtful discussion. I would answer people by making personalized video responses on YouTube and emailing them back. I would pick up the phone and call people to thank them for reading and chat about what they thought I should write about next. And this was when I barely had a readership—maybe less than five hundred email subscribers total. If you want to see examples of this, go to Rich20Some thing.com and scroll back to some of the earliest posts.

I responded to every single email until the day I physically could no longer keep up with the volume. And that took a few years. This was not easy work. I was specifically, purposefully, intentionally doing work that was NOT scalable. Yes, automation is part of the sales process when it comes to Internet business, but you'll never get the opportunity to sell to people if you don't first make an impression and build a relationship. It's up to you to cultivate that relationship.

I treated everyone not just as an avatar but as a person. Because, *duh*, that's what they were. It's easy to get obsessed with numbers when your business revolves around clicks, likes, and subscribers. But behind every one of those digital actions is a real, breathing human being who came to your work for a reason. And if you acknowledge that, you'll get the opportunity and the privilege of offering them something in exchange for money.

That's why they'll pick you. Not because you have the fanciest site (I didn't and still don't). Not because you are the smartest person (I don't consider myself a "guru"). And not because you're the most persuasive marketer on the planet (although I like to think I'm fairly convincing!). Not because of any of that—but because they feel close to you. The people at the beginning of your journey are your "ride-or-dies."

These are your one thousand true fans, and in the digital product business, this is often enough. Watch over these people carefully, because they will be the people who stick with you as you grow. As you gain more momentum and your audience expands, you'll begin to attract "tire kickers": people who just want to poke around, take some freebies from you, and bounce. Not everyone will be as engaged as they were before. But that core group, those one thousand true fans, will stick around and buy, time after time.

Now that Rich20 has grown to the point where I can't respond to every single email, tweet, and ping, I still operate with this mentality, but from a different approach. I created a private "readers only" Facebook community, to give my readers an outlet to support each other and to give myself an opportunity to be present in everyone's lives "at scale" so that they get a chance to know the real me. This is a key element to the success of our business, and I've found something very interesting as a result of starting that group. We have about 150,000 people on our email list as of this writing, and on any given day, our emails get about a 10 to 12 percent open rate. That means at least 15,000 people are reading each email.

And guess how many people are in our Facebook group? About 15,000. There's a very high probability that the people reading my emails largely consist of people in the Facebook community. This is why engagement is so important. In the beginning of your journey, go out of your way to meet your readers, fans, and followers, as you would new friends at school. Even when you have only ten people reading your work, learn everything you can about those ten people.

Another strategy I used to engage readers in the past involved a CRM (customer relationship management) tool like Highrise, essentially a database to track customer information. Whenever I had a conversation with someone via email and they mentioned a personal detail, I would make a note of it in the CRM and follow up with them later. If your birthday was coming up, I'd send you a quick email wishing you a happy birthday. If you mentioned you'd just gotten a new puppy, I'd email you in a few weeks and ask how it was doing, mentioning it by name! One reader emailed me and told me she was going in for gallbladder surgery in eleven days and was a bit nervous. I emailed her the day before to wish her luck and tell her I was thinking of her.

Who does this stuff? Nobody, that's who. And that's why they'll pick you when you eventually decide to sell something.

Something else to remember: Just because your customers buy another product from a competitor doesn't mean that they won't still buy a product from you, even if the product is about similar concepts. Would you buy only one book on marketing? Would you watch only one action movie? I actually encourage people to buy products online from all different places, and it doesn't worry me if they buy from someone else as well, because overall, I think it's good for the info product market. The more money people spend on digital products, the more normal it feels and the more money they budget for these types of expenses. Don't freak out. Just do you. Do your best work. Connect with your community, build a tribe, and treat them like family. That's how you'll get them to come back to you every single time.

Building the Machine

There's a very specific reason why I decided to save the actual how-tos for last, and it reminds me of my very brief tenure as a pickup artist.

When I was in high school, information products were just becoming a "thing." Even the concept of an e-book was revolutionary. *What . . . a book, that you read on your computer? Marvelous! Shall I print it out?*

Traditional marketers and old-school, Ogilvy-esque copywriters were still learning how to apply their knowledge from direct-mail and print advertisement to this newfangled online phenomenon. There was obviously money to be made, and, of course, one of the first niches to get real traction was dating. Since the beginning of time, guys have wanted to know how to get girls. *(I'm still working on it, actually. Anyway . . .)*

The big guy in the dating space at that time was named David DeAngelo, which was actually a pseudonym for the brilliant marketer Eben Pagan. His claim to fame was an e-book called *Double Your Dating*. When I saw there was a step-by-step guide to teach me how to get more girls, I was instantly sold. The only problem was, well, I was sixteen! I didn't have much money of my own, not to mention a bank account or a credit card. But what I lacked in money and financial structure, I made up for tenfold with determination and overall horniness.

At that time, you could still buy online products with a money order in the mail. So I scraped together the ninety-seven dollars—god knows how—and I rode my bike up to the post office to get a money order and send it to some sketchy PO box, hoping they would email me the e-book within seven to ten business days after receiving my check. That's a ton of money for a sixteen-year-old, but I really wanted to get girls.

As luck would have it, I finally did get the e-book, and I was hyped to start tearing through it. I was expecting to unlock a treasure trove of secret lines, body language cues, and ninja "make her wet with this one weird trick" techniques. Alas, I was sorely disappointed. Of the one hundred pages, the first eighty were devoted almost entirely to psychology and talking about things like "mind-set" and "limiting beliefs"! *I'm already taking AP psych, bro! I don't need another syllabus. Just give me the damn pickup lines!*

I wanted tactics! Unfortunately, that's where most people start, and stop, building their online business.

I get it. You want the juicy nuggets, the how-tos and the "do this" of actually making money—and we will, for sure, 100 percent, get to that. But first you have to understand the backbone of what you're doing. None of this makes sense, and it certainly won't make money, unless everything else is in line first.

So, that being said, let's talk about the core element of any info product business first: content.

Content: The Backbone of Your Business

We're in the vast blue ocean that is the Internet, and your content is the bait that brings three very important types of people to your work:

- **Fans:** the readers, listeners, and watchers of your work
- **Prospects:** the small percentage of those fans who may buy from you because your content is so damn good
- **Customers:** the prospects who "cross over" and become paying members of your community

It all starts with free content. Once people read, watch, or listen to your free content, they have the opportunity to become part of your little corner of the Internet, and it's this relationship that will be the backbone of your online business. I think the "free" part is what throws most people off. It's very easy to imagine that you should be compensated for every piece of material that you make. After all, you're putting hard work and effort into crafting the material, right?

Wrong. In today's oversaturated world, everybody knows that there's no shortage of free content. It all started with Napster in 1999. The idea that you could share music for free when you'd normally have to go to the record store was revolutionary, and ever since then, the public has had an insatiable appetite for free content. We stream music without buying albums, watch videos without buying DVDs, and read articles without buying a subscription to the paper. We expect free, and for the most part, despite the most valiant efforts of the world's big businesses, we've gotten our wish.

So how are you supposed to make money with your content or sell digital products if everyone has been conditioned to expect free work? Step 1 is to create incredible, world-class, way-above-average free content. Your content has to be so ridiculously good that it inspires the following thought in all your fans: *If THIS is what I get for free, what do I get when I pay?!*

And that's the mentality that will result in them buying from you when the time is right. Choose your medium to produce and the topic you want to discuss; there's so much to pick from. The type of content you should create is really dependent on how you like to express yourself.

I've always enjoyed the written word, so blogging made the most sense for me in the beginning.

Note: I'm intentionally NOT going to go too deep into the tech or setup for blogging, podcasting, or YouTubing in this book because that would be pretty overwhelming on the page, and I don't want to distract from the scope of the material. The main idea is getting an overview of what's going on and actually taking action with the knowledge you have at hand—not obsessing about the technology. If you're reading this book and have the ability to navigate Facebook and email, you are savvy enough to set up any of these systems.

Rest assured that everything you'll need to learn to set up a blog, podcast, or YouTube channel is specifically designed for beginners. These sites were designed with nontechies in mind. I'd recommend reading through this chapter, then googling or YouTubing any of the tech tools and terms mentioned here. You'll get a very clear understanding of how to set everything up. Conversely, if you don't feel like spending the time fiddling around, I've also developed an entire program to help you learn exactly how to launch and grow an online business, called Startup from the Bottom. You can get more info at www.StartupFromTheBottom.co. Plug over.

Blogging

Blogging started off in the late nineties as a way to keep a public journal of sorts and since then has extended to basically mean any type of writing published online. Individuals, groups, and businesses big and small have blogs. If it's written on a page in the form of a post, it's a blog. And yes, there are a TON of blogs out there already; some stats report north of two hundred million in existence. The caveat here is that most of these are inactive, as the owners abandoned them within weeks or months of starting, leaving a trail of mediocre, half-finished journal entries to litter the Interwebs forever.

But that doesn't have to be you. The main idea behind blogging (and all content development) isn't to come up with material that's never been thought of before. It's not to "break" a story, or be ranked number one in Google. Your objectives in writing a blog are to:

- Write something that's uniquely yours, from a perspective that only you can provide
- Create content that's extremely helpful to your readers and that's highly actionable (when possible)
- Produce work consistently to get people to come back to your writing

Compared to other mediums, blogging is probably the hardest place to find your "voice" in the beginning and to get into a groove, because of the simple fact that there's nothing to distract people from your content (as there would be with a podcast or YouTube video). It's just you, writing on a page. And in the beginning, your writing is going to suck. That's a guarantee. But after you're a few dozen articles in, you'll begin to find your flow.

Setting up your blog is pretty straightforward, and almost free. You'll need:

- A platform to write on. I prefer WordPress because it's free, it's the most customizable, and it's easy to set up quickly.
- A hosting service to place the blog's database on. I used Bluehost in the beginning. It's extremely easy to set up and very reasonably priced. I think you can get a hosting account for less than $3.50 per month.
- An email service provider so that people can subscribe to your newsletter, become engaged in your community, and, ultimately, buy from you. I'd recommend MailChimp as option number one, since it's free. But I also like AWeber, which usually costs about nineteen dollars a month for beginning users.

For a good example of how it looks when everything comes together, check out our blog at www.Rich20Something.com/blog.

Podcasting

Some people prefer to create and express themselves with audio content, which makes sense. There's something very intimate about speaking into a microphone and knowing that somebody out there is listening to your voice in the car, at the park, or while working out.

I think the most interesting thing about podcasts is that while traditional radio seems to be splintering and fading away a bit due to streaming music and other technology, podcasts are more popular than ever. When you start a podcast, you're basically starting your own radio show. You can do, say, or be anything you want, and you have the biggest platform in the world to find your audience with: the Internet!

You can run a professional-quality show entirely from your house, and since hosting the content on iTunes is free, you won't need to worry about supporting the broadcasts with advertisements (until you're ready to make more money, that is).

But there's a hidden networking power to podcasting. The number one advantage of podcasting is the ability to bring guests on your show. Nobody really highlights this, and I'm not sure why. When you invite guests on your show, you get to "pick their brain" in a way that just isn't possible on a regular basis. Imagine being able to connect with heroes, celebrities, and experts in your space; sit down with them for an hour; and learn everything about what got them to where they are. That's the power of the podcast.

As you continue to put out great content, your show will climb the rankings, and it will be easier to secure bigger and better guests. I've seen my friend Nathan Chan from *Foundr* magazine do it time and time again, interviewing megastar entrepreneurs like Richard Branson, Tony Robbins, and Daniel DiPiazza. It's probably the best way to meet people who are "out of your league."

Check out the Rich20 Podcast and subscribe so that you don't miss an episode at www.Rich20Something.com/podcast.

YouTube

People sometimes ask me what I would change if I could start all over again producing content, and I almost always tell them that instead of blogging, I'd probably start a You-Tube channel. Yes, writing tends to be the way that I naturally express myself—thus, the reason you're holding this book in your hands and not watching the *Rich20Something* documentary.

Still, I think that YouTube has the biggest potential for growth of all the platforms out there. For one, visual media is just rich; there's so much you can do with it. And videos tend to go viral a lot more easily. They are easy to share and fun to watch. But additionally, YouTube itself is a search engine. When you're trying to figure something out, one of the first places you look is YouTube, to see if somebody made a video explaining it. Video is also great for more artistic content, like music, dance, and spoken-word material. Just as podcasting is akin to starting your own radio station, YouTubing is akin to starting your own television station. And it's all free.

In Los Angeles, where I live, I constantly see billboards for popular YouTubers, which tells me that Google (which owns YouTube) is investing a lot of money into helping popular brands succeed. More and more frequently, we are seeing popular YouTubers transcend the Internet and move into more traditional media and movies, knocking down the gate-keepers that held the old guard in place.

And guess what? It's still free to start making this type of content. All you need is a laptop with a webcam and a free YouTube account. You can record the videos on your computer and upload them. Within minutes, you're up and running. Of course, you'll improve your content and upgrade your equipment as you keep going, but the point is that it's free to start. So what are you waiting for?

Check our the Rich20 YouTube channel at www.Rich20 Something.com/youtube.

Nav BK on the "Bigger Picture" Behind YouTube

As my YouTube channel, Absolute Motivation, started to grow, I realized it was bigger than me. It was about creating a place where people can go, in their darkest hour, and realize that they're not alone.

Nav BK

Founder of Absolute Motivation (with 350,000-plus subscribers on YouTube as of this writing!)

How to Produce Content That People Want to Read, Watch, or Listen To

The first decision you'll have to make is what you want to talk about. And this applies not just to written content, but to all content. What are you good at? What could you talk about enthusiastically for days from many different angles? It could be one thing or a collection of things, but find those core ideas.

For instance, the core idea and focus behind Rich20Something is helping young people live better lives by upgrading their wealth, health, and happiness. I use my own experiences to write about how you can make more money, become more well-rounded, and feel better about yourself.

This could take the form of:

- Step-by-step how-tos for starting a freelance business
- Case studies of successful readers and students who've left their boring jobs to become entrepreneurs
- Thought pieces on my philosophy behind improving your self-confidence and psychology
- Interviews with successful people
- "Ask the reader" pieces where I want to hear a consensus from my audience on a specific point or idea

Then, within those broader areas, I could even find different ways to talk about the same thing. For instance, if I wanted to write about how to start a freelance business, there are several different angles I could approach this topic from:

- A step-by-step guide to making your first thousand dollars freelancing
- Breaking down the biggest myths about self-employment
- Ten helpful tools for starting your freelance business
- How to raise the rates in your freelance business
- How to come up with a good idea for a freelance business
- An interview with three successful Freelance Domination 2.0 students

You can see that we're not reinventing the wheel here; we're simply looking at the same problem or idea from different angles. Some approaches are more appealing to people than others, so covering a topic from several different perspectives allows us to hit everyone in our potential audience.

To create content that feeds your online business (selling digital products), you'll need to keep two important things in mind:

1. Above all, you must be consistent. Since content is so easy and cheap to produce, you have to demonstrate that you're willing to show up every day, no matter what. Even before you're getting paid to do so—which could be for a while. Create a content schedule and stick to it. Without exception, I send out blog posts three to five times per week on Rich20, and have been doing so for years. If you want this to become a business, you have to treat it like a business.

2. You must include a call to action (CTA) back to somewhere that people can learn more about your ideas and sign up for your email list. In this business, collecting email addresses is EVERYTHING. In many cases, having a small, dedicated list of email subscribers is more valuable than a giant social media following or millions of eyeballs on a viral video. Your email list will allow you to capture the attention of your audience long-term, deliver value consistently, and create a relationship over time that will generate money for years to come.

Email Funnels and Sales Processes

Have you ever changed the oil in your car? It's a pretty basic skill that surprisingly few people actually know how to do. If you have, you'll most likely have used a funnel before. The main idea behind a funnel is to cast a wide net that you can pour the viscous liquid into without spilling it all over the engine block. The oil flows through the wide top end of the funnel and is neatly deposited into the narrow bottom end, filling your engine up so that the car runs smoothly.

In the Internet marketing world, we also have funnels. Their purpose is to cast a wide net and find people across the web who might be interested in our material, then get those people to neatly file themselves into our email database so that we can provide them with valuable content, market to them, and eventually make some money.

Getting People to Opt In

Once a member of your audience has interacted with your content, it's time to get them on your email list. This might seem challenging at first, but think about your own in-box. How many newsletters have you subscribed to?

The average person subscribes to anywhere between twenty and thirty different free newsletters from a variety of businesses—anything from a department store doing a semi-annual sale, to the Nissan dealership giving away insane deals on the 2018 Altima, to content-based emails about things that interest them. At one point, they weren't receiving emails from that business, and now they are. How does that happen?

In most cases, people sign up to an email newsletter to get something for free. This is called an "opt-in," and it's your bread and butter if you want to build an online business—especially one that's based on information products.

Getting people to sign up is relatively simple:

1. **Set up a basic landing page using WordPress.** A landing page is just a simple one-pager that offers something for free and has a place to input your email address in exchange for that free thing. Check out Rich20Something .com for a basic example. There are many different specialized softwares for helping marketers do this. Some of them are free; some of them are paid. As of this writing, Rich20Something uses two different software services to set up these pages: Leadpages and ClickFunnels.

2. **Create a free opt-in bribe to give away when somebody signs up.** This can literally be anything that you think might interest a potential customer. It could be a free e-book or checklist. It could be a few free videos on a topic that they care about. It could even be a complete mini-course to teach them a concept. All of these have worked well for Rich20 in the past.

3. **Drive traffic to the landing page to start collecting email addresses.** In the beginning, before you have a lot of traction, this will probably be your biggest hurdle. If you have a bit of money to play with, you can experiment with Facebook ads. But this is also where high-quality content really comes into play. The better content you make on your blog, podcast, or YouTube channel, the easier it will be to get people to check out your landing pages and sign up for

your email list. Great content creates better SEO, gets shared much more often, and naturally boosts your social media presence. This is where a long-game mentality becomes especially important, because the process will take some time. Focus on building up great content and consistently encourage people to go to your landing page by linking back to it whenever you produce a new piece of material. Make sure to give them a strong CTA, referencing all the benefits they'll get from the free download. In the meantime, use your existing social media to promote your work and start making connections with other influencers in your space. Over time, your following will grow, and it won't be hard to get more people on your email list.

Providing Value via Regular Content and Selling Your Material

Once people opt in to your email list, they expect to hear from you. So don't disappoint them! Now that they've given you permission to email them, impress the hell out of them on a regular basis with incredible free content in the form of blog posts, podcasts, and videos. In the beginning, you'll probably ramp up a bit more slowly; sending something once a week should be fine. But as you continue to grow, there's nothing wrong with increasing the frequency to several times per week. Generally speaking, as long as you're providing great content, people will want to hear from you.

The purpose of your content should be twofold: You want to provide something that genuinely improves your reader's life, but you also want to build up enough goodwill to earn the right to sell to them. There's nothing worse than people who have just met you and yet are already trying to hawk their goods at you. You have to start with some foreplay!

I started Rich20Something in 2012 and sent out content for over a year before I attempted to sell anything. During that time, I was getting to know my readers and determining the best way I could help them. I was trying to understand their needs and pain points, and building trust so that when I finally decided to sell something, they knew I wasn't some fly-by-night scamster; I was Daniel, the same guy they'd talked to and trusted for months. Even then, I didn't really get serious about turning Rich20 into a full-time business until late 2014. My readers had plenty of time to get to know me. This is the necessary work that you're going to have to put in if you want to be able to successfully sell a product online. Don't rush the process.

On the other side of the coin, remember: This is about business. You can't be afraid to sell. Some people will spend years writing content, doing podcasts, and producing videos, but are afraid to send a sales email because people might unsubscribe. This makes no sense.

Yes, the reality of sales is that not everybody wants to be sold to. But what's the point of building an engaged audience if you aren't going to monetize it somehow? You're spending valuable time to create meaningful work for people, and you deserve to be compensated for it. If some people don't want to buy—or even worse, they get upset and unsubscribe from your list—that's totally fine. You've just identified and smoked out the noncustomers from your community. Don't ever feel embarrassed or ashamed to charge for something that's designed to help people.

In order to sell people a product, you're going to have to engage them with a series of messages that pique their interest and speak to them on an emotional level. You should introduce the problem (or make them aware of a problem they didn't even know existed), then show them how your product could solve that problem quickly and painlessly.

To illustrate how this works, let's create a sample product. Something simple.

A Sample Week-Long Sales Sequence for Selling a Digital Course via Email

Let's say we're selling a digital course on how to play the guitar. Why did I pick that? Well, I just looked around the room and saw my guitar. But this doesn't even have to be an information- or course-based product. It could be a physical device or a service offering. The guitar course is simply an example. Use the framework and ideas here to create something unique based on what your audience wants and what you have to offer.

ASSUMPTIONS: We're going to assume a few things about our demographic and email list to guide our example. Do your own research for your market and email subscribers. For the purposes of this case study, let's assume our audience is:

- Primarily male
- Twenty-one to thirty-five years old
- Earning a fifty-thousand-dollar average annual income
- Native English speakers
- Inexperienced at playing guitar (either no experience or at a beginner level)

Following is a day-by-day bulleted breakdown of how the email sequence might play out. (I'm not going to write out the entire funnel for you because, damn, that would take a long time and you can't afford my copywriting services. But I'll give you enough to paint a clear picture.)

NOTE: As you start reading, you'll notice that I linked the skill of guitar playing to attracting women, because of the assumptions about my hypothetical demographic. This is an arbitrary decision I made because linking things to relationships, sex, or social pain can be powerful. You definitely don't have to take that type of positioning.

Monday: Emotional Story

SUBJECT: I watched from the sidelines as he impressed her . . .

- Emotional story about your high school experience. Relatable.
- One guy was so cool—always played guitar and girls swooned over him.

▪ Looked so rugged playing in the bed of his pickup truck. Held "parking lot concerts."

▪ He wasn't smarter or better looking than you; he just had a cool, in-demand skill.

▪ Pain of having no attention, not even knowing where to begin.

▪ CTA: Email me back—have you ever been envious of the attention somebody got because of a unique skill they had? Do you find yourself STILL thinking about it years later?

▪ PS: Tomorrow, I'll tell you exactly what I did to snap out of my "mental haze" and actually start learning guitar—and start getting more attention.

Tuesday: Overcoming Obstacles

SUBJECT: The moment I held my first Fender

▪ Narrator makes a decision that he's going to learn, no matter what.

▪ Goes into music store, picks up a Fender guitar.

▪ How it feels in his hands. He's inspired and a little afraid.

▪ But then, realizes that he doesn't have to master this overnight; it's a process.

▪ Crunchy tactic: Take learning a new skill one day at a time.

▪ Once I had this realization, a feeling of ease.

▪ Now I help my students get that same feeling, and it actually makes them see success much faster.

▪ Tease: If this sounds like something that'd be helpful to you, keep reading. I'm working on something special that I'm going to reveal tomorrow.

Wednesday: Sales Email 1 (Soft Open)

SUBJECT: Finally . . . it all started to "click"

▪ Narrator starts playing, slowly, painfully, but progress is there.

▪ Starts to learn one of his favorite songs, and actually gets it!

▪ Not 100 percent confident, but brings the guitar to school, where the cool guys are.

▪ Starts playing and attracts a little crowd.

▪ Girl he likes says, "OMG, I love that song!"

▪ He can't stop smiling, and at that moment, it "clicks."

▪ He realizes guitar isn't about the instrument; it's about self-improvement and expression.

▪ His confidence is up 1,000 percent, and he keeps learning and getting better.

▪ Why did he wait so long?

▪ Now, he wants to teach other people how to have the same amazing feelings, so he developed XYZ course.

▪ CTA: I'll be telling you more this week, but if you're sick of waiting for this transformation, you can check out the course here.

▪ LINK TO COURSE.

▪ PS: Course will only be open until XYZ. Add LINK.

Thursday: Sales Email 2

SUBJECT: XYZ course is now open—learn more here

■ Yesterday I told you about my turning point, blah blah blah, and now I want to tell you about the course I put together to help you get there even faster.

■ Here's a tactic/strategy you didn't know.

■ List features of the course.

■ List benefits of the course.

■ What if you had this? How much better would your life be?

■ CTA: Click here to join the course. LINK TO SALES PAGE.

■ PS: Tomorrow is the last day. LINK TO SALES PAGE.

NOTE: The difference between features and benefits: Features tell what the product does or consists of; benefits tell how it will help or change the user's life.

For example:

■ **Feature:** "Ten hours of modules in HD video, plus weekly emails to help you."

■ **Benefit:** "Learn to play your favorite song two times faster than you could trying to teach yourself."

Friday: Sales Email 3

SUBJECT: Is XYZ course right for you?

- Identify all objections and prove they are wrong.
- This course is right for you if . . .
- This course is NOT right for you if . . .
- "Future-casting": Where will you be six months, one year, five years from now if you don't take this step?
- Testimonials from current customers, if you have any.
- Guarantee.
- LINK TO SALES PAGE.
- PS: Scarcity: The course is closing Sunday—get it now! LINK TO SALES PAGE.

Saturday: Sales Email 4*

SUBJECT: XYZ course is closing tomorrow!

- Hazards of not taking action (doom and gloom!).
- Examples of people who were skeptical but for whom it worked!
- Challenge yourself. You have nothing to lose.
- This is the last time you'll hear about this for a while.
- Brief recap of benefits.
- LINK TO SALES PAGE.

* Sometimes a personal video works well with this pitch. Just open up your laptop and speak openly and honestly.

Sunday: Sales Email 5

SUBJECT: Last chance to get XYZ course!

 ▪ Last-chance scarcity.
 ▪ Emotional call to action, reminding them of what
they could do with the material.
 ▪ Brief and to the point.
 ▪ LINK TO SALES PAGE.

I should stress that this is a simplified version of a sales
funnel. Some sequences last for a few days, some for a few
weeks. The duration and content of what you write will depend greatly on your level of experience, your relationship
with your list, the price of your product, and many other factors, but the core elements are there.

First, build your relationship with your subscribers.
Spend time nurturing your list and building a community.
Figure out what you can sell them. If you're not sure, simply
send them an email and ask them, *"Hey, I'm thinking about
making a product about XZY—is this something that you would
be interested in?"* Then use their answers to decide whether
your idea is worth pursuing.

If you want to be even more confident, you could presell
the product first, before you even make it. Send your readers
sales emails first, see if people actually buy, and only make
the product if you can turn a profit. The biggest validation of
your idea is somebody actually pulling out a credit card and
purchasing it. This is a no-lose scenario for you, because you

won't have to lose time or money making something that people don't want, and you can do this ethically by refunding people if you decide not to go through with it.

Building Your First Information Product

So what type of product should you build, and what should go in it? It all depends on how much time you want to put into the material and how much you would like to charge for it. Generally speaking, the more interactive the content is, the more you can charge. As you become more skilled at copywriting, marketing, and positioning, you'll learn how to enhance your presentation to charge even more.

Here are five types of products, what elements they might include, and the approximate price point you might charge for something at that level. We're not going to bother naming what the actual product would be here; that's not the point. The point is to give you an overview of the possibilities and a good idea of the potential for what products can make at each level.

Product Type 1: *The "Tripwire" or Self-Liquidating Offer*
Price Point: *Anywhere from $1 to $50*
The "tripwire" is fundamentally an impulse buy that a customer won't think twice about buying. It should provide a simple solution to a basic problem. Typically, it's one of the first offers that they see from you; sometimes it's even offered directly after the user signs up for your email list, on the "thank you" page (thus, the term *tripwire*). This type of offer is great if you are running paid advertising to your land-

ing pages, because if even a small percentage of people who opt in end up buying, it will pay for some or all of your advertising expenses. Some experts also say that these offers are great for "conditioning" users to buy more from you later down the road, since they already feel a sense of security, having bought from you once before.

Typically this type of product is just a short e-book or a handful of basic videos explaining a topic.

Product Type 2: *Entry Level*
Price Point: *Anywhere from $100 to $300*
Entry-level products are relatively low-cost, but still highly valuable. They are designed to solve one or two very specific pain points and generally aren't comprehensive, but they are in-depth enough to be appealing. At the higher end of this range, the profit can really start to add up. For instance, if you sold a hundred copies of a $297 product over the course of a year (about two per week), that would be an additional $30,000 in revenue. Not bad! The material for this type of content can be PDF and/or videos. And you don't really even need to place products of this caliber inside a special membership platform.

Product Type 3: *"Bread and Butter"*
Price Point: *Anywhere from $300 to $500*
"Bread and butter" products are the go-to for many online marketers. The price point is a sweet spot between affordable for the customer and highly profitable for the business. At the higher end of this spectrum, the customer usually expects some type of membership platform that they can log in

to. Products of this caliber could include audio, video, and text. The subject matter usually encompasses more material. Many info product businesses subsist off products in this category alone.

Product Type 4: *Flagship*
Price Point: *Anywhere from $500 to $2,000-plus*
These products are premium. They should cover an entire topic from top to bottom and include a wealth of material, and they are almost always hosted on a membership back end where students can log in to access, download, and ask questions about the content. They'll typically provide HD video, as well as audio and text components. In some cases, there will even be a live component that includes webinars with interaction from an instructor to supplement the material. They are more expensive, so they tend to be a major purchase for the customer. As such, customer support needs to be really good, and you'll need to work harder to sell courses of this caliber. But when you figure out the formula for selling courses at this level, both you and the customer win.

Product Type 5: *Recurring Subscription*
Price Point: *Anywhere from $20 to $100 per Month*
Recurring products or "membership" products are designed to provide continually updated content to the user every single month. The main purpose of these products is to consistently create something new that users will want to access on a regular basis. Just as with a gym membership or your Netflix subscription, you continue to get billed while you continue to use the service.

While the initial price point on the product seems small, the recurring revenue per user really begins to add up. For instance, at fifty dollars per month, the average user will spend three hundred dollars after just six months, but the effect will feel negligible compared to spending $50 up front. This gives the user a much lower barrier to entry, while giving the business consistent month-to-month revenue. Typically these sites also have a membership back end where the user can log in, and the content can be any mix of material.

The Membership Back End

At some point you're going to have to actually make a product. It's not as hard as you might think. Almost all info products can be made with simple, consumer-friendly software that is easily managed, like WordPress. It's not like building an app or something else that requires more involved programming; there are many inexpensive WordPress template options out there, and you can use them to create high-quality, professional-grade digital products that look like they cost thousands to make. You'll even be able to password-protect your content so that noncustomers cannot access the material. If you can set up your website in WordPress, you can build your first product.

Rich20 uses a software called SamCart to accept payments. It is easy to set up and get running immediately. We use WordPress plug-ins called OptimizePress and ClickFunnels to build everything from tripwire to flagship products. They are inexpensive to purchase, offer great functionality, and look very professional.

Quick Recap

The new American dream is to make money while you sleep. And at the risk of sounding like a late-night info-mercial, I can tell you that this is entirely possible. However, the myth of passive income is that it's easy. It's not. It requires a ton of hard work up front, and it might even be years before you see truly passive income, where you check your email and find that you've literally made money while sleeping. There are lots of different ways to make money online—it's not just through selling your old stuff on eBay—and that's because we've moved through the agricultural age and the industrial age and we're now in the information age. The information age is great because, yes, everybody can be a content consumer and, yes, everybody can become a content producer— which is exactly what you need to do to start your free-lance career, and start your online business, and become a full-blown entrepreneur. Something else about making money through an online business: It's not magic; it's math. If you have only ten subscribers, ten people caring about your business, then get to know those ten people. Reply to their emails, ask them questions, take an interest in them. Because that's exactly what everybody else won't do (it's not scalable, and it takes up too much time, and whatever other excuse they want to use). Doing this will separate you from your competition, and when the time comes for you to release your own product, your "true fans" will be excited to buy from you.

Notes from the Field

Will Mitchell, Founder of StartupBros

I met Will years ago, way before I had any idea how "serious" either of our little blogs would become. I remember thinking, *Oh, hey, here's another person from my hometown (Tampa) who is writing online. We should be friends.* Little did I know I was talking to a mogul in the making.

What's so incredibly striking about Will is his utterly relentless drive to build his company, StartupBros, into a business that genuinely helps thousands upon thousands of young entrepreneurs figure out how to get started. In that way, our missions are very similar.

But Will has also taught me the incredible value of working tirelessly for a cause that's bigger than myself. He is so fiercely dedicated to the success and happiness of his clients that it's made me completely rethink the way I do business.

When I grow up, I want to be like him. You should too. Check out more of his work at www.StartupBros.com.

The only thing I've had to sacrifice is everything. Entrepreneurship is all-enveloping, and the best entrepreneurs are fiercely dedicated to their mission. Every entrepreneur you meet has sacrificed a "normal life" to become what and who they are today.

But if I had to do it all again, I absolutely would. It's a crazy and wild ride, but it's the only ride for me.

I knew I was going to be an entrepreneur when I was

seven years old. My parents were poor when I was born, but they worked hard and took risks, and sold a business for a huge sum just a couple of years after they started it. The thought of it thrilled me: out there on my own, making magic, risking everything to change the world. I was hooked.

The most difficult part of my journey has been believing in myself. Entrepreneurship really is a beautiful way to discover more about who you are and what you need to develop. If there's something you need to improve about yourself, or if you find it almost impossible to handle situations, there's nobody to answer to but you. It's a lifelong journey to rise above the nonbelievers—and that includes yourself.

I almost gave up when my parents told me to quit what I was doing and go to college. It was tough for me to stand up to my father, because I respected him more than anybody in the world, but I stood my ground because I knew that what I was doing was the best way to be a successful entrepreneur. He didn't support that decision, and that made me realize that entrepreneurship really is a journey that you take alone.

The first thing you must do when starting a business is simple: sell. Lots of people like to "play business." They like to set up websites, come up with names, get a logo, file to become an LLC, tell all their friends about how excited they are—and exactly none of that is going to grow your business. For example, I employ a cleaning service. This cleaning service has no logo, no website, no business cards, and it doesn't even have a name! So what do they have? They have amazing relationships with their clients. It sounds so simple, but so many people screw up here.

One thing that people need to start a business that they don't know they need is extreme confidence, but without the ego. You need to know that you're the best person for the job while realizing that you're probably clueless and need to keep learning and adjusting all the time.

It's fashionable to say "never give up," but I entirely disagree. Part of being an entrepreneur is knowing when to quit and try something new. But you must never quit based on emotions or feelings; you must only quit when the business model isn't working. And if it's not working, that's OK. Never get too attached to an idea. There are millions of them.

I think, to be an entrepreneur, you need to be addicted to achievement and success. Real entrepreneurs aren't in it for the money. Lots of entrepreneurs make their first million and then lose their minds because that goal they were working so hard for has been accomplished, and they hadn't thought beyond that.

Do I think anybody can be an entrepreneur? No. You need to be able to handle extreme levels of stress without flinching. You need to be able to ride financial roller coasters that would drive most to suicide, and you need to be able to ride them more than once. Being an entrepreneur isn't glamorous, and I just don't think it's right for everyone. It's for people who value a life of ultrahigh risk and ultrahigh reward.

PART III

The Growing

How to Build Your Network,
Your Knowledge, and, Most Importantly,
Yourself

9

Real-World Networking: How to Make Friends with Influential People and Level Up Your Life

The richest people in the world look for and build networks;
everyone else looks for work. —Robert Kiyosaki

You can make more friends in two months by becoming
genuinely interested in other people than you can in two
years by trying to get other people interested in you.
—Dale Carnegie

KEY TAKEAWAYS:

$ Nonlinear networking is about you offering incredible value, not asking for incredible value.

$ Do not ask, *"How can I help you?"* Do your research and find out how you can help them. DO ask, *"Who else should I be meeting who's cool like you?"*

$ People will think you're lucky, when it's actually just consistency.

> $ Persist—because that's why this book is in your hands right now.
>
> $ The essential components of real-world networking: offer value, be interesting, be interested.

OK, let me clear the air for a minute.

For the past eight chapters, I've been teaching you how to overcome mental barriers, get focused, and start a business—both online and offline. I've given you examples to consider from history, pop culture, and my own experience.

I always felt like there was something a little "off" about getting advice from people who have already had a high level of success in their field. Consider a supermodel like Gisele Bündchen. She's one of the most beautiful humans on the planet. She's married to Tom fucking Brady and has been the highest-paid supermodel in the world consistently for over a decade. Whether you're gay, straight, black, white, or orange, there's no denying it: She's hot.

But if you were to ask her about how to become a supermodel, I doubt she'd be much help. It's not that she's unintelligent or lacks a wealth of experience in the field. The problem is that, well, she was already born equipped with the "tools" for the job. Her face, her body—those are just genetics. She was discovered at fourteen by a major modeling agency while she was at the mall on a school field trip. That's not really something you can replicate. If anything, it just seems like luck or destiny.

And that's the problem I was running into when writing this book. I've tried starting a bunch of things. Some of them have worked; some of them haven't. But as the years progressed, more and more of my attempts have succeeded. From the outside, it might seem a little unfair, or perhaps it looks like I'm consistently getting lucky.

But here's the key: I couldn't have done any of this on my own. I credit much of my success to my network of influential friends.

Let's back it up a few years . . .

In college, I wanted to start a magazine publishing company. My idea was to create one of those cheap circulars with bits of free content about health and fitness, supported by ads from local businesses that wanted to promote to our audience of primarily college students and get more foot traffic for their stores. Keep in mind, this was in 2008, exactly one year before the launch of Groupon and a ton of other daily deal apps. Not exactly what I would have called "forward thinking," but hey, it could have worked!

One of the first places I looked for advice was the local SBA (Small Business Administration) office. Most major cities in the United States have one. Their job is to advise new business owners on which steps to take next and—once in a blue moon—give out a few loans.

My friends and I sat down with the SBA adviser assigned to us, and we eagerly told him our revolutionary idea. He didn't seem too enthused. Then, he pulled out a giant book full of statistics for businesses in every possible industry. *"L . . . M . . . N . . . O . . . P . . . publishing, here we go."*

He scanned down the page with his index finger, wrinkled his brow, pushed up his glasses, and then flipped the book around so that we could see it.

"Yeah, this is a pretty tough industry, guys. You're going to have a really hard time."

I don't even remember exactly what statistics he showed us, but essentially it amounted to this: We were fucked. He didn't say that outright, but we caught his meaning.

"Is there ANY advice you can offer us that might give us a better shot?" we asked.

He told us to start networking and getting our name out there; then he handed us a stack of flyers for different local mixers, meetups, and networking events we could go to. Over the next few months, I went to a LOT of these events, and I learned one thing: They were completely and utterly useless.

The last event I went to was on a Sunday morning at a broken-down diner called Whistle Junction. The group was about forty people. We all sat at tables in a crooked semicircle and went down the line like on the first day of middle school, introducing ourselves and telling everybody what we were working on. I say "working on" because most people in there hadn't made a dollar at their business. We were all "wantrepreneurs" who had probably gotten advice from the same guy at the SBA. The coordinator of the meeting instructed us to get up, grab some microwaved meatloaf, and "mingle."

I went from person to person collecting business cards. A carpet cleaning company. A tree removal service. A landscaper. How were any of these "connections"—with other people who were struggling as much as I was—supposed to help me launch a magazine publishing business?

I was annoyed, to say the least.

When I found out the fee to be part of this incredible

group was $450, I excused myself to the bathroom and ran to the car.

Networking sucks! I thought. And I'd be damned if I was going to sit there and eat crusty, reheated meatloaf with these weirdos every weekend. I was definitely lost, and didn't know how I was supposed to meet people who could actually help me launch my ideas. All the wisdom tells us that it's about who you know—and I knew nobody.

Fast-forward a few years later, and things are much different. My network has exploded. In my group of friends, I'm fortunate enough to have celebrities, best-selling authors, TV personalities, and megasuccessful, multimillionaire entrepreneurs. Having these types of friends has changed everything. They've opened countless doors for me and helped me make hundreds of thousands of dollars and, in all honesty, they are the reason I'm even able to write this book.

But here's the funny thing: I didn't deliberately try to "network" with them. What I've learned over the last few years is that you're not going to meet influential people at Meetup .com mixers. They're not there. They are too busy hanging out with other influencers in a room at an upscale restaurant that you didn't even know existed. And they aren't charging each other $450 for the privilege of meeting. They are helping each other make deals and meet other high rollers on a regular basis, because they understand that when their friends do well, so do they.

I call this "nonlinear networking" (NLN).

The main idea behind NLN is that you're not going to make all your connections in an obvious, straightforward fashion. If you want to do business with Oprah, emailing her your pitch probably has a zero percent chance of success. But perhaps through a convoluted series of three or four connections, you meet one of her producers at OWN and get invited to a party that she happens to be at. Well, now your odds have improved greatly.

Other people will hear your story and say, *"Wow, you're so lucky you got to meet Oprah!"* But you'll know that meeting her was just the end result in a chain that probably started with a much smaller connection.

Nonlinear networking requires that you educate yourself, improve your character, and offer tremendous value to others so that instead of having to hunt down the people you want to connect with, you naturally become somebody that people want to help. The main focus is to build a "curated" group of friends who all share a common thread.

Rather than being a spoke in someone else's wheel, you'll become a hub. Over time, with this approach, you'll see how even small connections can turn into huge wins for you— both in your business and your personal life.

Having a powerful network often seems like luck to the outside observer partly because there is no real step-by-step process. I can't hold your hand and tell you who to talk to— or exactly what email to send. This is a process that you'll have to feel through, and sometimes it might feel like you're bumping around, blindfolded in the dark. It won't be a copy-paste solution. So instead of trying to fit the process into some artificial mold, I've decided to just tell you my story.

I'm going to share the wild story of how I exploded my brand, caught the attention of the major media, and eventually landed a publishing deal that resulted in the very book you're reading right now. It's your job to take notes along the way as I deconstruct my approach and see how these lessons apply to you.

You're not going to be able to replicate exactly what I did. And you shouldn't want to. I'm me. You're you. We are in a different time and place. But I can guarantee you this: What I've done is not particularly special or hard to match.

Above all, be patient with this process. It's not supposed to happen overnight—and that's the point.

IT ALL STARTED with a *pop*. I'm not quite sure what I was doing up so late, but I think I was deep in a Reddit rabbit hole when I ended up at the Art of Charm.

Art of Charm's entire focus is on helping men develop social skills, confidence, and charisma in business and life, and their podcast boasts over two million listeners every month. As Ron Burgundy might say, they're kind of a big deal. That's why I was so surprised to hear from the cofounder on my first visit.

As I was browsing articles and videos one night, I heard a little *pop* and saw a chat box appear on my screen.

"Hey, I see you're checking out AoC. Can I help you find something?"

I was a bit taken aback. *Great, one of those robotic customer service agents*, I thought. But I decided to play along.

"Are you even a real person?" I asked.

Then I looked at the name; it was Jordan Harbinger, the cofounder and main radio personality on the podcast. Usually when a business grows large enough, the founders aren't manning the customer service desk, so this surprised me. We started chatting, and he seemed very cool, easy to get along with—and he didn't try to sell me anything.

Jordan was in the airport, en route from Hong Kong to Pyongyang, North Korea, for a sightseeing trip, so he didn't have much time to talk, but even from our brief conversation, I got the impression that this was a guy I wanted to know. He was young, successful, and doing something that I wanted to do. He interviewed celebrity guests for a living, ran a million-dollar business, and got to work from anywhere in the world. I didn't know exactly how I'd be able to get into his "circle," but I wanted in.

Fast-forward six months, and I was preparing to make my move from Atlanta to Los Angeles. My girlfriend had some family out there, but I knew nobody—except Jordan.

I wanted to make a natural, nonsleazy connection with him, because even though I didn't know much at the time, one thing I did know was that making friends with influential people is one of the fastest ways to become influential yourself.

So rather than thinking about how he could help me, I began thinking about how I could help him:

- What could I do for him that he would find useful?
- Who did I know that I could connect him with?
- What could I offer to move his business forward?

Something worth noting here is that I didn't email him and say, *"Hey, Jordan, I really want to get to know you. How can I help you?"* This is a well-intentioned, albeit incorrect approach that many beginning networkers make. If you want to connect with an influencer or VIP, the last thing you want to do is ask them, *"How can I help you?"* I get emails like this all the time now from readers who want to get my attention, and my first thought is, *"I don't know! You tell me!*

Asking someone how you can help them forces them to stop what they're doing and think of things for you to do without knowing anything about your skills or background. As the person seeking the connection, it's your job to figure out how your skills would be most useful, and that will require you to do some independent research to find out exactly what the VIP might need!

When I thought about what Jordan might need, the first thing that came to mind was publicity. Every business needs good press—especially podcasts, which depend on finding more and more listeners online.

How could I get the Art of Charm podcast more attention, traffic, and listeners? Hmm . . .

Then, eureka!

My friends Matt and Jared owned Under30CEO, a huge website for young entrepreneurs that I'd done several guest posts for and had gotten a fair bit of traffic from. I knew that I could connect Jordan with Under30, get him a guest spot, and help him drive some traffic back to his podcast. It was worth a shot. I shot him a quick email.

Subject: Let's get AoC in front of three million people :)

Hey Jordan,

Hope all is well and you're not detained in a North Korean jail cell!

I'm a frequent contributor to Under30CEO and good friends with the founders, Matt and Jared. The site gets about three million unique visitors a year and has a really en-gaged audience. I've gotten a lot of new readers from them!

I was thinking of a few ways AoC might be able to collab-orate with Under30 to help blow you guys up and bring tons of new listeners your way.

I just moved out to LA a few weeks ago. Want to grab some sushi and discuss? I can come close to wherever you are!

Talk soon,

DD

Jordan got back to me later that day, and it was on for the following week!

Worth noting here: This email worked because it was straight to the point and offered a clear benefit to Jordan. In-fluencers and VIPs are busy people, and this approach won't always work. Sometimes people won't have time to meet with you, and that's OK. I could have easily made the introduction between Jordan and Under30 with a simple email. As you use this approach more often, however, it will eventually lead to more and more connections, and those connections will make future meetings much easier to get. Focus on offering a clear benefit to the VIP, and don't sweat the small stuff.

The next week, we sat down for sushi at a restaurant in West Hollywood, and it was chill. I'd just moved out to Los Angeles and was generally impressed by anything LA. We talked online business, which I was still very much a neo-phyte in, and generally felt each other out.

I learned more about what AoC was doing, and we brainstormed some ideas for interesting content collaborations they might be able to do with Under30CEO. I connected Jordan and Under30's cofounder, Matt, to each other via email while we were still sitting at the table. It was a great lunch.

As we were getting ready to leave, I asked him a question that has become one of my core networking strategies to date. You should ask this question whenever you meet an influencer. It's the ultimate network expander.

I said, *"Hey, man, this was really great. Who else do you know in LA who's cool like you? Who should I meet?"*

This is a deceptively powerful question because it achieves multiple objectives simultaneously:

- It affirms the meeting you just had was great.
- It compliments the influencer.
- It subtly encourages the VIP to introduce you to other influencers without exactly asking him or her to do so.
- It allows you to consistently grow your network of interesting friends who are doing cool work.

Think about it: If you ask people a question like *"Who do you think I should meet?"* when they respond with a name, the natural next step is for them to connect you to that person. They wouldn't suggest someone who they weren't comfortable introducing you to.

Although the questions often achieve the same aim, there's a massive difference between asking *"Can you introduce me to ____?"* and *"Who do you think I should meet?"*

The former is framed as a favor because you're asking the influencer for something. There is a certain amount of "social capital" needed for these exchanges, depending on how big the ask is, and if your relationship with the influencer is still new, you might not be in a position to make such a request.

There are a lot of considerations that go into introductions, and the biggest concern for influential people is introducing someone else to an important contact and possibly damaging the relationship in the process.

On the other hand, simply asking people *"Who should I meet?"* is an innocuous question that doesn't necessarily require influential people to make an introduction if they don't want to. It's not a direct ask. It allows VIPs to "scan" their mental database of contacts and handpick a few people who they think might be a good fit with what you're doing and where you are with your life, without the potential awkwardness of them having to deny you an introduction. It's phrased in a way that allows them to offer you something of their own accord, so it doesn't really feel like any social capital is being expended by either party.

I asked Jordan who I should meet, and he introduced me to his friend Gabriel Mizrahi via email. Gabe is a writer and filmmaker in Los Angeles around my age doing some really cool projects, and Jordan thought we would hit it off.

A few weeks later, Gabe and I met up for coffee. No business—just two people meeting for the first time. And here's the cool part: Since we were introduced by a mutual friend, there was already a certain level of rapport and good vibes between us. You'll find that when you meet friends of friends, there're usually already some shared values between you. You'll have things to talk about immediately and will probably share at least a few viewpoints on major issues. The more you network in this way, the more curated your friend group becomes, until eventually you are surrounded by awesome people.

Gabe and I had a good "man date" and kept in touch over the next few months. But that's not where the nonlinear networking thread ends. Not by a long shot.

A FEW MONTHS LATER, I had the opportunity to interview prolific inventor and multimillionaire investor Lori Greiner. You probably know her from the wildly popular ABC show *Shark Tank*. After some relentless follow-ups with her PR team, I scored an in-person interview for her then-new book *Invent It, Sell It, Bank It!* I was pumped! This was going to be huge for my brand as a thought leader, and I was really looking forward to meeting her in person. Talk about leveling up!

But there was one problem: I had nowhere to conduct the interview. I was stressing out! Here I was with this gigantic opportunity and nowhere to interview her! I started calling anybody and everybody I knew in Los Angeles (maybe seven people total at that time) and asking them if they knew any nice locations where I could interview her for free or cheap.

Nobody had any good places in mind—until I called my friend Gabriel Mizrahi, the talented screenwriter in Los Angeles.

As it turned out, Gabe had just gotten hired by a television studio in Beverly Hills called TheLipTV. They had a full studio. It was a possibility. He introduced me to the owner, Michael Lustig, an interesting guy—extremely smart, straight to the point, and not afraid to tell the truth. I explained the situation to him, and he said, "Sure. Come on in and interview her here. You can use the entire studio after hours. For free."

And just like that, I was in.

Connections are powerful. It only takes one yes from someone to change the entire trajectory of your life, and this yes from Michael proved to be one of those moments. Later that week, I got in the studio with Lori, and things went very, very well. I thought that would be the end of it, but Michael was impressed. He offered me a job hosting my own show, right on the spot!

I was floored. Try to keep up with the flow of events here:

- I'm on Reddit, probably looking at cat pictures. I find Art of Charm.
- Jordan pops up in a random chat bubble.
- Six months later I move to LA and meet up with Jordan. He introduces me to Gabriel.
- Gabe and I meet; he introduces me to Michael.
- Michael lets me film in his studio for no apparent reason.
- I now have my own TV show.

None of these seemingly disconnected events lead to each other logically or linearly. If I'd tried to go through the "front door" and attempt to get in front of Jordan without offering something first, it wouldn't have worked. Then I never would have met Gabe.

Without Gabe, I never would have met Michael, and the TV show never would have happened. You're not always going to be able to plan exactly how you'll network your way to the top. It doesn't work like that. The only thing you can do is offer consistent value—like I did for Jordan, Gabriel, Lori, and Michael—and with consistency, other people's circles will open up to you. Networking isn't something that you "do"; instead, you have to become somebody that people want to have in their circle.

And the chain didn't stop there. My show on TheLipTV brought a ton of awesome opportunities. I got paid to hang out in Beverly Hills and interview celebrities, athletes, authors, and even porn stars. Well, actually, only one porn star. Had to stop doing that. The girlfriend was NOT pleased. It was an awesome experience.

Soon into my tenure, I had the opportunity to interview best-selling author Stephen Key. Like Lori, Stephen is also a prolific inventor, and his book *One Simple Idea* was an enormous success. Our interview went well, and we struck up a fast friendship.

One day, he shot me a quick email: *Hey Daniel, my editor at* Entrepreneur *magazine is looking for more contributors. Are you interested in writing for them?*

I'm sure you can guess what my response was: *Hell yes.*

And just like that, I became a featured writer, which blew up my brand and my business and led to my getting spots in all the major magazines, including *Fortune, Inc., TIME,* and *Business Insider.* Things were really starting to pick up.

Stephen became a mentor of mine, and we talked regularly. Eventually he asked me, *"Hey, have you ever thought about writing a book?"*

I responded that of course I had thought about it, but I didn't want to self-publish and didn't even know the first step in getting started with traditional publishing. I'd heard it was very hard to get the attention of agents and publishers. It seemed like getting a "real" book deal was near impossible for a nobody like me.

So Stephen introduced me to his agent, Kirsten. Kirsten is a very successful agent at a major New York literary agency. She specializes in celebrity books and works with a lot of actors, thought leaders, and entertainers—people whom you've definitely heard of. With a simple email introduction, Kirsten agreed to a phone call with me.

Agents are the key to getting in front of major publishers and getting your book into stores, but let me be clear here: You do not simply get a phone call with a major New York literary agent for no reason. In most cases, they don't even read unsolicited manuscripts. It's a closed circle in many ways. It's notoriously, intentionally hard to get their attention. Yet here I was, on the phone with her.

She heard my idea for *Rich20Something*—the very book you're reading right now—and said she liked it. She was concerned I didn't have a big enough following to interest publishers, but that wasn't a flat no. It was enough to light the fire under my ass.

Over the next year and a half, I worked my tail off writing hundreds of articles, doing interviews, and building my social media following and my email list. Every few months, I'd email her:

Hey Kirsten,

Hope you're doing well. Here's what my social media is at now. Here's how many email subscribers I have. My audience is growing fast!

Or . . .

Hey Kirsten,

I just launched a product, and we made fifty thousand dollars in a week! I bet I could do the same for a book!

Typically, she wouldn't respond, and I expected that; I was simply updating her on my progress. But one day in July 2015, everything changed.

I'd been aggressively growing my platform for months, and I was finally starting to see real results. Here's what I sent her:

Hey Kirsten,

Hope you're doing well. When we first started talking last year, you'd expressed interest in my book idea, but you suggested that I work on building my platform first. I've been working really hard for the last eighteen months, and I've built something that I know will be a perfect platform to sell a shit ton of books. And the best news is, it continues to grow even more every day. **Here's a brief recap.**

Last time we talked, my website was getting about 13,000 visits per month, my email list was about 5,600, and my social media was negligible.

As of July 2015:

1. My email list is nearing 50,000. *We are averaging 700–1,000 new email subscribers per day, and are on a steady pace to finish the year with between 150,000 and 200,000 email subscribers. That's a LOT of potential book buyers waiting to be emailed!*

2. My website traffic has skyrocketed from 13,000 to almost 90,000 per month.

3. My social media is really blowing up—*especially Instagram, where I just passed 75,000 followers. I'm growing at a rate of 1,200 per day and am on track to be at over 250,000 followers by the end of the year. But the best part isn't just the following; it's my organic reach and engagement. My posts average 2,500 likes, and when I ask my followers to do something, they do! For example, when I asked them to comment on certain posts, those were flooded with more than 850 comments in a few minutes.*

4. I've developed relationships with and secured columns in all the best outlets, and have seen several articles go viral. *My advice is regularly featured to millions of people all over the world through my new columns in* TIME, Fortune, Entrepreneur, Huffington Post, Fox News, *and* Business Insider.

The piece in Entrepreneur *got over 40,000 shares on Facebook in under a week. The one in* Business Insider *drew almost 400,000 readers. I just got into* Inc. *and* Forbes *as well!*

FYI, I'm not just listing those links to show you how much of a big shot I am (although my mom thinks I'm one); I mention them because after writing for many big outlets, I've

*learned how to craft pieces that SPREAD, and I can repli-
cate this for our promotional campaign. Plus, I can promote
my work in these columns.*

 *Anyway, I hope that these are the types of indicators you
were looking for. If you're still interested in discussing a
book, I'd be more than open to it.*

Looking forward to speaking soon!

Daniel

As soon as I pressed "send" on this, I immediately for-
warded it to Stephen, saying, *If this doesn't secure a book deal,
I don't know what will.*

And can you guess what happened? She replied. Quickly.

We got on the phone that week and closed the deal. We
immediately started working together on my proposal, and
within a matter of months, we'd landed a deal with the biggest (and, in my humble opinion, the best) publisher in the
world, Penguin Random House.

And now this book is in your hands. Who knows what
this book will lead to next for me. More importantly, where
will its ideas lead *you?*

No matter where you go from here, what I want you to
take away from hearing my experience is that it all started
with a chat bubble on a website. Networking is so much more
than just meeting people. Becoming a good networker is really about building a life that other people want to take part
in because you're giving them what they need. And you'll get
so much back in the process.

Brad Cameron on Giving Incredible Value

Something I never thought I'd have to know that's ended up being crucial to my success is how to build a powerful network. I believe that your network is your net worth, and that relationships are crucial to building and growing your business. Always find a way to deliver value to your business friends, and always give value first. Eventually, it'll come back around. For example, I promoted Daniel on my Instagram page, and he taught me a ton about building the back end of a business, and now I'm being featured in his book. Win-win!

Brad Cameron

Founder, Build Your Empire

www.BuildYourEmpire.co and on Instagram at @buildyourempire

Connecting the Dots

Caution: The story I've told in this chapter is not meant to be a blueprint or a how-to. It's more like a postmortem or a debriefing of why things worked out for me.

So what can you learn from all this?

One of the things that bothers me the most about talking to people about networking, connections, and success is that if you've accomplished a lot, people often look at the achievement and not the root of that achievement. Nobody looks at the "why" behind it all. So let's zoom out for a minute.

How does high-level networking really happen? How do

you meet people and make the connections that will dramatically change your life? Through friendships. Real, genuine, "I like you and you like me" friendships. Yes, there are the circle-jerk chronic networkers who want to climb their way to the very top of the social ladder. But nine times out of ten, that act is transparent. People of value see through that charade instantly, and after some time, most of the social climbers are banished from the ranks of influence.

You should always try to make genuine connections with people and help them. It should be coming from a real place. There's always give-and-take, and oftentimes, the give comes without the expectation of immediate return. For instance, months after Stephen introduced me to my agent, Kirsten, I got my work featured in *TIME*. Who do you think the first person I introduced to the *TIME* editors was? Stephen didn't ask to be introduced to *TIME*, but I was so grateful to him that it was a no-brainer. I had to repay him. And so the circle continues.

You shouldn't be out to serve only yourself, but you CAN be targeted about how you form your relationships or who you reach out to. It's OK to find people who you'd like to connect with (or who are a direct connection to other people you need) and specifically get into their world in order to eventually be in a position to make an ask—whether that ask is a connection, a piece of advice, or even an investment. When it's the right time to make that ask, you'll know. You'll have a good sense of how much "social capital" is stored up in your bank.

Your job is to be the real you, to offer genuine value, to

come with good intentions and tools to help influencers who you would like to know better. Figure out what they need and want without asking them; then deliver it to them. After a few years of doing this, you'll become the type of person who people actually want to help without even asking. You'll be getting the "hookup" all the time.

Once you become a bit more influential in your space, it's very important not to be stingy with your connections. Oftentimes, as we get a little more traction, we start to hoard connections and withhold introductions from one person to another because we don't want to damage our relationship with an important person. This notion is false, which is a good lesson that I learned from Stephen Key.

If you are friends with someone (even a new friend), you trust them, and they've demonstrated good character so far, then there's no reason why you shouldn't introduce them to your influential friends. Stephen didn't have to introduce me to the editors at *Entrepreneur* magazine, and he especially didn't have to introduce me to Kirsten. But he understood that helping me to grow my network also helped to grow his. Now that I've gotten more exposure due to his help, I can return the favor to him tenfold.

Another important factor, which Michael at TheLipTV taught me: Aim high and take risks. The worst that somebody can say is no. Even very famous people may be fewer connections away than you think. When you're reaching out to people, you never know who might respond. I had every reason to believe that Lori Greiner would not respond to my interview request. After all, she's a rich celebrity and I was just some "no-name" blogger. But even rich celebrities have needs you can fill. In her case, she had just released a book and needed the publicity. My offer to have her in studio was exactly what she needed at that time.

Never count yourself out because you think someone is out of reach. Instead, try to figure out what they need and how to reach them with that.

Three essential components of real-world networking:

1. **Offer value:** Have something going for yourself; a skill or talent you can provide that will help someone is a must. You gotta be GOOD at something. Skills pay the bills.

2. **For the love of God, be interesting:** Have a project that you're working on, something that you're actively creating to make the world different from how you found it. Read more books so that you have interesting things to talk about. Don't expect to be a "do-nothing bitch," as UFC star Ronda Rousey would say, and expect to get ahead.

3. **Be more interested in other people than yourself:** Actually care about other people and what they are doing. Don't just call people when you need something, and don't just suffer through other people, waiting for a pause so that you can get your two cents in. Eighty to ninety percent of your conversations should be OTHER people talking about themselves. People will LOVE you for it and listen to whatever you have to say when it's time.

Quick Recap

Networking requires that you offer incredible value. That's how you'll meet the people you really want to know, rather than the people who spend all their time going to "networking events." And when you reach out to those people, never ask how you can help them. They don't know you, they don't know what skills you have, and asking them how you can help them has now forced them to think about what you can help them with! Do your research, and offer value where they need it. Once you connect with them—in person, if possible—ask them who else you should meet who's like them, because it flatters them, and it's a way of getting them to introduce you to their influential friends without you explicitly asking, *"Hey, can you introduce me to all of your most influential friends?"* When you start networking like this, people will think that it's all luck. But the real key is to offer value at every stage. Always think about how you can help the person. That way, you'll become someone who people want to have in their circle. That's real networking. And when it comes to getting an incredible opportunity because of your network, you still have to persist. I spent a year and a half sending emails to my literary agent, Kirsten, updating her on my progress. Imagine if I'd stopped, if I'd given up, if I'd decided it wasn't worth it! You wouldn't be reading this book.

Notes from the Field

Jordan Harbinger, Cofounder and Radio
Personality at the Art of Charm

Now that you know the "long story" of how Jordan and I met, and how that one relationship changed the trajectory of my career, it's only appropriate that he tell his story here.

Just think: If it wasn't for him (and many other people along the way), you probably wouldn't be reading this book! You can check out more good stuff from Jordan on the Art of Charm podcast in the iTunes store or at www .TheArtofCharm.com.

I started the Art of Charm because I wanted to help other people overcome social issues like anxiety, not knowing how to network, not being able to influence people. But then it became more about hacking our brains, because I realized that this was the biggest competitive advantage. It's hard to make yourself significantly smarter, and of course you can outwork people, but there's only so many hours in a day. Charisma, personal magnetism—these are teachable skills. And I want to bring them to the whole world.

One of the most important sacrifices I've made is not having the choice of passing responsibility to someone else. It's my business. There's nobody else. It's all on me. And saying that, I'd absolutely do it all over again. I sometimes ask myself if I'd have the guts to do it all over again, knowing how hard it's been, but I think I would. I'd just love to do it and not make all the mistakes I made.

I did come close to giving up. About six years ago, on more days than not, I'd wake up and think that I just wanted to work at the post office. It seemed like such a predictable job, one where I'd have no worries. Or I'd drive by construction sites and think about how they got to work outside, in the sun, and leave off at half past four. And I felt myself envying it. There were so many stressful things happening in the business—people stealing from us, for example—and I longed for simplicity.

Obviously, I didn't give up; otherwise you wouldn't be reading this right now. Instead, I persisted. I persisted for a few reasons. First, I didn't know what else to do. Second, I loved the mission even though I hated the day-to-day for a while. And third, we started getting more and more emails from clients telling us how we'd changed their life. So even though I hated it for a while at the time, I knew I was doing important work.

Something I never thought I'd have to know that ended up being crucial to my success was learning how to study other people. The Art of Charm takes top performers and dissects what they do, and then we teach it to our audience. So I feel like some sort of X-Man: I try to get everybody's unique superpower. It's been crucial to my success because it's become what the Art of Charm is all about.

Something else that's contributed to my success is my delusional confidence to execute, overcome things, and succeed. I want to be the best interviewer in the world, and I know it's possible. I see other people—people on TV, people who are legends in the industry—and I know I can be better than them. I know it. But—and this is important— I combine my delusional confidence with a ridiculous work ethic. I know I can get to the top, and I'm actually working to get there. If you have delusional confidence but don't have a ridiculous work ethic, then you're probably expecting things to happen to you without making them happen, which is real delusion.

If I could go back and say something to myself on the day I started my business, I'd say this: Don't hire your friends. That might sound easy and obvious, but when you need someone to do a hundred-thousand-dollar-a-year job for twenty-five thousand while sleeping on your couch, who else is going to do that but a friend? Those are the people that trust and believe in you. Nowadays, thankfully, it's kind of cool to work at a start-up, and you can find interns and people who would be willing to take a discounted salary for the chance to build something.

I want to run my business for the rest of my life because it's a legacy business, not a lifestyle business. Lots of people like lifestyle businesses because they want to have passive income, and travel around the world, and learn to surf—and that's OK. But that's not me. I've got something to deliver—the ability to unlock brilliant people's brains and share the results with the world—and it's going to take a lifetime to do it.

10

How to Keep Growing: Mental Tools and Strategies for Daily Living

I do think anyone can be an entrepreneur, but then it
does seem to take a certain type of personality, and it's a
personality that includes the most entrepreneurial trait
there is: the ability to persist.
—Steve Chou
    Founder, My Wife Quit Her Job
    www.MyWifeQuitHerJob.com

IN CHAPTER 2, I suggested that instead of spending time and money working on a degree you might not use, you could do meaningful activities to help you find your life's work. One of those activities might even include writing a book. Of course, any book written early on in your life is only going to reflect your experiences up to that point. Looking back on that book years later, you might feel like the younger you had a lot to learn.

I must confess, even reading this book back now, I feel

the same way. Just a few years ago, I was so hungry. I was desperate for change, and I would have done anything to get out of the daily grind. It was eating me up inside. I remember staying up until all hours of the night, reading voraciously, trying to figure out how to get from where I was to where I wanted to be. It was all I thought about.

I started to see some results. At first I was completely elated. I went from minimum wage to six figures, then from six figures to seven figures, using the exact mental strategies and business ideas laid out in this book. Then something interesting happened: I felt trapped again. I was shocked to find myself feeling so dissatisfied when on the outside it seemed like I'd gotten everything that I wanted.

It wasn't until very recently that I realized that whatever level of success you achieve becomes your new "set point." However much money you make becomes the new status quo. If you travel the world frequently, that becomes normal. After you buy your first luxury car, it just becomes your everyday car. As you're reading this, you're probably thinking, *Yeah, yeah . . . I've heard it before. Money doesn't buy happiness. But I'd like to find out for myself.* And I'm confident that with the strategies in this book, plus some good old-fashioned hustle, you will soon see this for yourself. But trust me when I tell you that the hedonic treadmill never stops. In fact, the time you're happiest will probably be the very moment *before* you get what you've always wanted; that's when the anticipation and the desire are at their highest point. Life is all about foreplay. Once you get it, well, you got it. On to the next one.

So will happiness always evade us? What's the solution to not only getting what we want but actually being satisfied with our lives? Well, I may be able to give you a more definitive answer on my ninetieth birthday, but for now, I think I have an idea: constant, intentional growth and self-development. You have to adopt a growth mind-set.

Growth feeds your soul, gives you a worthy target to aim for, and gives you a reason to celebrate when you've done a good job. Focusing on growth in all areas of your life also forces you to make mistakes and confront yourself honestly, which is possibly one of the hardest things anybody can do. There have been times when I would have rather confessed to capital murder in front of a grand jury than be honest with myself about a personal shortcoming. Know what I mean?

As the months and years go by, it's imperative that you examine your beliefs and really dig into not just the whats in your life, but also the whys, so that you can better understand your own actions. Once you do this, you can begin to develop your own set of core values to guide your actions. Like an oath or a code of honor, your values should reflect the concepts in your life that are most important to you. You should refer to them whenever you need to make an important decision, and default to them whenever you're unsure of which road to take.

I've developed seven core values for my own life that keep me focused on growth. They're simple phrases that I say to myself every day, and they help keep my eye on the bigger picture. I'd like to share them with you here. Feel free to take what fits with your life and adapt it as you see fit. I hope these maxims help you as much as they've helped me.

Seven Maxims for Growth

Maxim 1: "I can always improve." There's always something you can do to be better. To be a better entrepreneur. A better son, sibling, friend, or partner. A better human. A better self. There might be times when you are haunted by mistakes in your past, and you mistakenly equate yourself with them. It sounds corny, but every day you wake up is an opportunity to change. And the decision to make these changes starts with a single choice.

Maxim 2: "I persevere when I am frustrated." Resilience is in short supply these days. I blame the Internet. Because everything promised is easy. Because everybody wants things now. The world has been around for over four billion years. Modern civilization has only been here for about six thousand. Don't rush the process. Things necessarily, and without exception, take time. While that time is elapsing, don't give up because you're frustrated. Persevere. Consistency compounds like interest over time.

Maxim 3: "I don't run from mistakes; I learn from them." Hear me now: You are supposed to make mistakes. Every single piece of human knowledge is the result of an initial failure. Every book that's been written, every idea that's been thought, every invention that's been made—all were created to solve a problem because somebody, somewhere, made a mistake. Mistakes push us forward. If you're categorically avoiding them, you're not risking enough to reap big rewards. Rather than being afraid of making mistakes, look at them as necessary rites of passage, discard the anguish, and retain the lesson. Then help other people to avoid the same traps.

Maxim 4: "I am inspired by people who succeed." I think we all have a subtle tendency to conflate admiration with a bit of haterism and self-doubt. At least, I know I did this for a while. If we see people (especially friends or family members) who are doing better than us, we come up with subtle reasons to passive-aggressively tear them down in order to bolster ourselves in our own minds. It's a defense mechanism to protect ourselves from feeling bad for not having the same results in our own lives, and it works wonderfully for a time. For example, if some entrepreneur friends of mine had an epic product launch and I was jealous, I'd think to myself, *Yeah, that's really good. I'm so happy for them! They just spend so much time working, though. I really prefer to be more balanced in life.* See what I did there? It's very subtle.

Instead of looking for subtle reasons to invalidate the accomplishments of others, we should be inspired by their success. In fact, of all the emotions in the human spectrum, I think jealousy is the most useless. When somebody accomplishes something that you'd also like to accomplish, the question you should be asking is not Why are they better than me?; it should be How can I do the same? Once you have that mental shift, you'll be able to focus much more clearly on growth, and you'll eliminate a ton of subconscious negativity in your life.

Maxim 5: "I can learn anything that I want to." I was watching the movie *Divergent* the other day. I can't remember who's in it, except for Zoë Kravitz (for obvious reasons—Zoë, call me!), or what the movie was even about. But I do remember one interesting point: Every person in this society has a particular predesignated role. Some people are selected to be warriors, some to be intellectuals, some to be farmers. On and on it goes. And there is no opting out. Whatever you were designated to be, that's what you're stuck with. I can't help but feel like our education system is the same way.

From a very early age, we are told by our parents, friends, and teachers that we are good at some things and not at others, sometimes blatantly, sometimes much more subtly. But the indications are very clear, and over time we start to believe this and identify with it. I was always a reading and writing kind of guy. I excelled at anything literary very early, and because of that, those traits were reinforced. My teachers would cater to my strengths. My parents would reinforce them by saying things like, "This family doesn't really do well at math." And for a time, I thought there was something truly different in my brain that made it harder for me to understand more left-brained, mathematical concepts. Thus, I became what the evidence supported. My test scores were always crazy good with anything involving reading or writing, while my math scores and science scores were mediocre at best.

Once upon a time, I was even a premed student. After failing chemistry, I thought to myself, You know what? This is something that I'll just never be good at. Now, I know that is complete horseshit. It wasn't that I couldn't do chemistry; it's simply that I didn't care about it. It didn't inspire me. Nothing in the medical field did. Deep interest is the key to acquiring elite-level skill. Think about it: When you are really interested in something, doesn't that make it easier to learn? Your brain is incredible, and anything that you want to become good at is within your realm of natural abilities. Nothing you need to learn will ever require a genius-level IQ, from rocket science to starting a business. You just need the right approach, patience, and, above all, confidence in yourself.

Maxim 6: "I can make a difference with my effort and my attitude." My high school guidance counselor, Mr. Garcia, had one of those awesomely cliché motivational posters in his office with an eagle soaring high in the sky, and it said, "Your attitude determines your altitude!" And despite the fact that Instagram has almost completely destroyed the meaning behind inspirational quotes, this one still rings true.

The way you perceive things influences the way that they turn out, and those results in turn influence your beliefs. It all starts with you and your attitude. This is similar to what's called the "observer effect" in physics, whereby the very instruments used to measure a phenomenon alter the phenomenon itself. You are the instrument! This means that you must guard your thoughts accordingly. If you continually focus on why something will be too hard, the task will seem that much harder because you are magnifying the hard stuff. If you focus on why something is possible, why you'll succeed, why a task will be enjoyable, you'll experience those effects much more profoundly. After a short time, you'll come to realize that in many cases, events are just events, and the impact they have on our lives is almost entirely chained to how we understand and perceive them.

This slightly dispassionate worldview is a core component

of Stoic philosophy, which I've deeply integrated into my life. This isn't to say that emotions don't sometimes take control, but rather that when they do take control, you must learn to step outside of the fray, look at what's happening to you objectively, and make an active decision to change your behavior, despite how you might be feeling. When you change your behavior and your attitude, you will greatly influence the outcome of whatever obstacle you are dealing with.

Maxim 7: "I like to challenge myself." Just like our tendency to avoid mistakes, we often avoid challenges, because challenges usually lead to error. Or psychological strain, which is painful and unpleasant. But avoiding challenges is trading long-term fulfillment for short-term safety.

By and large, the very nature of challenges is that they start off difficult and become progressively easier. Along that path, you learn both the skills you need to succeed at your discipline and the person you need to become to rise to the occasion. I've learned this in nearly everything challenging I've ever done, from jiujitsu to learning how to solve a Rubik's Cube. Through continuous challenge and with relentless persistence, frustration always gives way to understanding. And then competence. And finally, mastery.

So my prescription for you is to intentionally, actively seek things that will challenge you. If you understand everything in your life, you're doing it wrong. There should be at least one element of your day that frustrates you enough to lead you to constantly seek a solution. It could be something like a complex business problem, or something simple like reading a book that's above your comprehension. Begin to see challenge and confusion as an indicator that you are on the right path, rather than a sign that you should turn back and head toward more familiar territory. Stretch yourself. A mind once stretched will never return to its original shape.

Jill and Josh Stanton on The Journey

The biggest excuse we had to overcome before we started was that we didn't know enough. Who were we to charge for this stuff? And why would people pay? That stopped us before we even had a chance to start. If you ever feel like we did, remember this: Everybody started somewhere.

Would we do it all again? Hell yes. In a heartbeat. Because our entrepreneurial journey has been the best form of personal development we could've had. We're not who we were when we first started out. We're more patient, supportive, and strategic, and that's just a few examples. Also, our marriage is so much stronger, because we're building our dream together and we believe in each other. And we'd absolutely do it all over again just to have the perspective we have now.

Jill and Josh Stanton

Founders of Screw the Nine to Five

http://screwtheninetofive.com

What Got You Here Won't Get You There

As your beliefs about yourself and your abilities change, so too should your habits. The habits that got you to where you are today most likely won't get you to where you want to go next. Now, creating better habits is a subject for an entire book's worth of material, but I would like to share with you a few insights that have helped me improve my day-to-day life tremendously. Of course, all the ideas in this book are interrelated. But if you can only make a few small behavioral changes in your life immediately, I'd recommend starting here.

Read More Books—a Lot More

You're at the end of this book, so hopefully that's an indicator that you already like reading. However, if you don't, I must take a second to emphasize its importance. In school, we were conditioned to just take reading like any other medicine. It was just information that we had to absorb in order to regurgitate. Most of the pleasure, mystery, and utility was stripped away from it.

But think back just a few hundred years. Most people could not read at all. Only members of the clergy, politicians, and aristocrats were able to read—and even then, books were scarce. In some cases, only one copy of a book existed in the entire world. Books were regarded as serious treasures because they contained the sum total of another human being's experience in a given area, which allowed others to progress much more quickly. The written word still remains one of the best (and certainly one of the oldest) ways to see inside somebody else's mind and understand their thoughts. If you're solving a problem, there's almost a 100 percent chance that somebody else has already solved all or part of it and written the solution in a book. There's a reason why Bill Gates and Warren Buffett read fifty to a hundred books a year.

If you want to start a business, there's simply no excuse to be clueless anymore. Imagine the fact that a world-class expert can work for thirty years to figure something out, completely devoting her entire life to one particular question, and you can get all of her knowledge on that subject in a two-hundred-page book that can be read in a weekend. Consider the fact that you can have access to this information for pennies on the dollar by simply going to Amazon and buying a used copy. There is no excuse anymore; you have access to the information.

It goes without saying that there is also a ton of information online, and books aren't the only place to learn. After all, I spent an entire chapter discussing how to build an online course to teach other people things. But there is something elegant about the self-contained portability of a book that will always make it attractive. And some of the world's greatest minds existed long before the Internet, so you'll have to read their works the old-school way.

Whatever you choose to read is fine. Fiction feeds your creativity; nonfiction feeds your knowledge base. Biographies of people you admire give you insight into great minds. It's all good. Whatever you choose, I recommend sticking to a schedule and committing to feeding your brain at least some sort of written material for thirty minutes a day without fail. This is especially important for content creators, as the best way to come up with creative ideas is to synthesize them from the ideas of others. I do not view reading as a leisure activity. It's serious work, and it takes effort. I often don't "feel" like reading, but just like brushing my teeth is a part of my physical hygiene, reading is part of my mental hygiene. It just has to happen every single day. No exceptions.

There are a few books that, among a sea of others, I view as essential "ground zero" books for anyone looking to level themselves up, start a business, or change their lives. If you're new to this whole "serious reading" thing, I suggest you start with one of these.

Do yourself a favor by going on Amazon and picking up a copy of all these. You can get them used; I don't care. Just do it. Don't argue with me.

Here they are:

- *Mastery*, **by Robert Greene.** Greene is also the author of the best sellers *The 48 Laws of Power* and *The Art of Seduction*, but I think *Mastery* is by far his best. The book crystallizes lessons from the world's most prolific artists, scientists, and entrepreneurs, then distills their teachings into actionable insights.
- *Scrum*, **by Jeff Sutherland.** *Scrum* will completely redesign the way that you look at your life—and more specifically, your to-do lists. This goes way beyond productivity advice and creates a fundamental shift for you to get much more done in much less time. Good for both teams and individuals.
- *The Art of Learning*, **by Josh Waitzkin.** Waitzkin is the chess prodigy about whom the movie *Searching for*

Bobby Fischer was created. He's also a world champion martial artist. In this book, he breaks down everything he's discovered about how to learn more quickly and how to go from average to elite in any discipline.

- *Deep Work*, by Cal Newport. Taking all the above books into account, Newport, a professor at Georgetown University, synthesizes the concept of focus. Why is it that some creatives and professionals can get volumes of work done at a high level, while others can barely manage to get anything done at all? Does society just need more Adderall, or are we misunderstanding some fundamental ideas about focus? Cal goes deep.

- *The Hard Thing About Hard Things*, by Ben Horowitz. Ben Horowitz is the cofounder of Andreessen Horowitz, one of the most well-respected venture capital firms in the world. But before that, he was the CEO of Opsware, a software company that was all but doomed to complete devastation. This book details all the mindsets he had to adopt and the man he had to become to turn the company around and exit with over $1.6 billion.

- *Meditations*, by Marcus Aurelius. Aurelius was one of the great emperors of Rome, known to many as the "Philosopher King." But despite being the most powerful man in the known world, he struggled with all the same things you and I do. This book, which was never supposed to be published, is a journal of his thoughts on struggle, adversity, and dealing with pain. It's a cornerstone of Stoic philosophy and puts all of life into perspective.

Start Meditating—Immediately

I was never that in touch with my spirituality. You're not going to find me sitting cross-legged in the garden or doing sun salutations in the park. I've always enjoyed things that were more fast-paced, and if given the choice, I'll usually choose something that's intense and exhausting over something that forces me to sit and reflect.

But I can say unequivocally, that meditation, changed my life.

I tried in the past to get into it, not because I wanted to but because I heard that other successful people were doing it. I never quite understood the purpose. What was I supposed to do? Just sit there and "focus"? Focus on what? How? I'd sit on the ground with my eyes clamped shut, trying to visualize something. All the while, my legs were cramping and falling asleep. Most days, my mind was racing all over the place, and I was simply counting down the seconds until I could get up. Other days, I'd just fall asleep. Not very inspiring.

But as my business began to grow, things got a lot more hectic. I had so much mental chatter that during the day, I'd find it nearly impossible to get anything done. I felt a bit like Cyclops from the X-Men without his special glasses. My brain was a powerful laser, but without the proper tools, I couldn't direct its focus. As a result, my energy went everywhere, and I diluted my own effectiveness. This was extremely stressful because the primary tool I use for my business is, you guessed it, my mind! I need to be able to direct my thoughts!

So I reluctantly tried the whole meditation thing again.

But this time, instead of simply doing it because other people thought it was a good idea, I decided to do my own research and figure out what the goal of meditation was supposed to be. I learned that it's not about being Zen or finding enlightenment. It's not about having a completely clear mind, or even about having some particular insight. It's only about mindfulness.

Being mindful simply means being aware of your thoughts and having the ability to observe and direct them. Take a second to think about a typical thread of your own thoughts. How might it originate? Perhaps you begin working on a project and get a text message. You check the text message, and your friend has just sent you a funny video. The video is hilarious, and sparks a chain reaction where you end up watching five more (they're only three minutes long, you tell yourself). After those videos, you're kinda off center, so you check your email to remind yourself of the important work tasks that you should be doing. You see an email from someone asking you for something that makes you anxious. That anxiety builds, and now when you get back to the project you'd originally started, ninety minutes have passed, you've lost the thread, and you're feeling upset emotionally.

How many times has something like this happened to you? Just raise your hand silently. The problem with this scenario is that it's an all-too-common example of lack of awareness. Every step of the way, you're taking actions, but you're not making conscious decisions. You don't have the ability to step out of the chain reaction and then observe and redirect your own thoughts to take you where you want to go. As a result, you end up somewhere completely different from where you want to be. The more this happens on a day-to-day basis, the less control you feel over your actions and your life.

Meditation resolves this problem by training your brain to focus your energy, just like lifting weights trains your muscles to pick up increasingly heavier weight. After you begin meditating you'll start to notice something interesting: The distractions will still come, and you'll still get pulled by them, but when they start to pull you too far down the path, your brain will say, *Hey, get back to center.* As if a GPS were guiding you down the road, you'll be able to get back on the main route, even if you take a few side streets.

Outside of focus, another place where mindfulness and meditation really shine is emotional control. Oftentimes, we don't even realize how far out into the emotion ocean we've gone until it's too late. It's easy to start layering emotions, tangling them into an indecipherable web that ends in exhaustion. Something happens that upsets you. Now you're angry. You snap at a friend or loved one. Now you feel ashamed. Next, you're annoyed at yourself for feeling ashamed. On and on it goes. Meditation practice gives you the tools to step outside of this and look at yourself more objectively, then catch yourself before the emotions take over and tangle everything up. If I feel myself getting angry or sad, the mindful approach allows me to look at the situation like a third party, removed from the situation, and say, *Daniel is beginning to feel angry. Don't let this affect how he treats others.* It sounds strange to think of yourself that way, but this is the approach that will allow you to make active decisions in how you feel and what you do, rather than be dragged everywhere by your emotions. This will allow you to become much happier, calmer, and more effective in almost every area of your life. Meditation and mindfulness just make you a better person.

To get good at meditation, like anything, you have to train yourself consistently. But the good news is, you don't have to spend hours at a time doing it. I typically meditate once in the day, usually in the morning, for ten to thirty minutes, depending on my mood. You'll want to start with some guided meditation to help cultivate this new skill in your life. I recommend the Headspace app, which is an amazing tool, full of guided tutorials that teach you the purpose and process behind mindfulness and meditation. The sessions are short and to the point, and you can choose different "packs," which are designed to address specific areas of interest.

Accountability: Get Some

At this point, I hope you realize that the most critical element to success in any endeavor is consistency. Where you focus the bulk of your attention and time is where you'll see the biggest results. But even highly motivated, consistently focused people need someone to keep them in check. I recommend getting an accountability partner or a coach.

If you've ever tried to work out at the gym consistently, you know there's a big difference between going alone and going with a training partner. On the days you go alone, the only person you have to report to is yourself. Workouts are rarely as intense, and if deep down you don't really feel like going, you can make up an excuse not to. I've done it thousands of times. But introduce a training partner into the mix, and what happens? Now, every time you go, you want to put in your best effort. You push a little bit harder because someone is there looking out for you. And if you don't feel like going, now you have to come up with an excuse to tell your partner, which always feels lame. Just the presence of somebody else holding you accountable for your goals makes it easier to get things done.

The same is true in other areas of your personal and professional lives. Can I tell you a little secret? Without my accountability coach, Adam Reed, this book probably wouldn't have been written—or at least it wouldn't have been done anywhere near on time. Adam, who I hired through an amazing service called Coach.me, had one task and one task only: to make sure I sat my ass down and wrote every single day. All of a sudden, because I had someone checking in on me, I was much more effective. I began to build the habit of daily writing because I knew he would hold me accountable. We even created consequences if I didn't hit my daily word total. Without this added leverage, it would have been too easy to slack off.

The great thing about accountability buddies or coaches is that they force you to do the things that are important but not urgent. So often we spend our days in reactive mode, putting out fires rather than executing on our long-term vision. We think we're doing the really important work, but month after month, our big projects are stalled. An accountability buddy can help you see this roadblock for what it is and overcome it.

Start by figuring out the number one thing that you should be doing but that somehow always gets pushed to the side to make way for more "urgent" things. Maybe you need to be studying for a major exam to get into grad school but have so much schoolwork that you never get around to it. Maybe you need to be making more sales calls to grow your business but have so much existing client work that you never find the time. Whatever the issue is, find a friend (or hire a coach) to keep you accountable and then watch your rate of success rise rapidly. If you want to get massive leverage on yourself, pledge a certain amount of money to an organization you hate, hand your accountability buddy a check, and force them to donate the money if you don't follow through with your end of the bargain. That should get your attention! And if you miss your goal once, I bet you'll never miss it again!

IF YOU MADE IT THIS FAR, you're awesome and I love you. And I want you to know one thing: **You can do this.**

You honestly, truly can. I used to read books like this when I was finding my way, and my thoughts about them were always the same: *Yeah, it worked for him, but I just can't see it working for me.*

Now I know, more than ever, that the playing field is level. No matter where in the world you live, no matter if you're a man or a woman, no matter if you're black, white, purple, or green—you have the tools and the intelligence to take your life and your destiny into your own hands. It all begins with your decision to do so and your commitment to put in the time, day after day—especially during the hard days.

I'm not some mystical voice from the ether. I'm a real human, sitting here in a chair, writing something that I hope you'll love.

If you loved the book and it helped you, I'd love to hear from you. If you have questions, I'm here for those too. You can reach me at **Daniel@Rich20Something.com**. I'm only a few clicks away.

I've also put together a ton of free resources for you, including never-before-seen videos and free downloads, at **www.Rich20Something.com/bonus**. Check that out ASAP!

Until then, keep pushing. Thank you so much for reading! I'll talk to you soon,

DD

Resources and Recommended Reading

You know what ROI is, right? Return on Investment. But what about ROT? That's your Return on Twenties.

Rich20Something is more than a book—it's a movement. Our entire mission is to help you get the biggest return on this critical decade of your life. Your twenties are important because they help you set up the rest of your life—and I want you to look back on your life in ten years and smile because you know that you did everything you could to make this period of your life incredible.

It's time to make more money, make more friends, and have more adventures. Here are a few places you can go to get started:

www.Rich20Something.com: This is our main site. You can get all the latest updates from the Rich20 team on leveling up your life. Make sure to check out the blog, podcast, and all the new videos that we drop weekly!

www.Rich20Something.com/bonus: Claim your free bonuses as a thank-you for purchasing the book.

www.FreelanceDomination.com: This is where the hustle begins. Whether you're still working your nine-to-five and just want to make an extra thousand dollars on the side, or you want to scale up your existing service-based business, this is the place to start. Thousands of successful students agree!

www.StartupFromTheBottom.co: If you've been struggling to put together the pieces of starting a successful online business, this is your opportunity to learn the step-by-step process from experts who've been there before.

And, of course, there's always me. Have a question? Email me: **Daniel@Rich20Something.com**.

Or, feel free to hit me up on social media:
Instagram: @Rich20Something
Facebook: Rich20Something
Snapchat: @Rich20Something
Twitter: @Rich20Something

Acknowledgments

I'd always known that it took more than one person to write a book—but I never really understood what a collective effort it was to get one out into the world until I had to do my own.

Since every experience I've had up to this point has led to me writing this book, I really have everyone who I've ever encountered to thank for the inspiration behind this work. But that would take a bit too long.

To my incredible parents: You embody the meaning of unconditional love and support. Thank you for being a model of integrity and compassion. I love you!

To my wonderful girlfriend, Sara: Thank you for being my rock. A tremendous partner, a constant sounding board, the voice of reason, and the keeper of my secrets. I'm honored that I get to spend my life with you. It's a privilege to be loved by you. Thank you, thank you, thank you. I love you always.

To Stephen Key: Thank you for introducing me to this crazy game. You're a friend for life!

To my superagent, Kirsten Neuhaus: You literally willed this book into existence. I am forever grateful to you. This is only the beginning. Thank you!

To my editor, Stephanie Bowen: Your diligence with my baby, support through the process, and attention to detail has made all the difference in the world. Thank you!

To DT and Alicia: You two have become two of my closest friends and have been the missing element in my life that I'd been looking for but didn't know I needed! Here's to years of friendship, fun, and growth.

To all my friends, family, and, most importantly, to my TRIBE: At the end of the day, this book is here because you asked for it! It was possible ONLY because you found something relatable and real in my writing—and I'm grateful every day for you. I hope I get to hug every single one of you over the course of my life.

Much love and appreciation to life for this gift!

DD

Index

About the Author

DANIEL DiPIAZZA is a millennial business guru and the young entrepreneur behind the massively popular career and lifestyle website Rich20Something.com. He has successfully started three consecutive freelance businesses and scaled them to over a hundred thousand dollars in revenue with zero start-up capital. He has over 204,000 followers on Instagram and 16,000-plus Twitter followers, and has been the subject of interviews and feature articles in many national media shows and publications. He is the author of the popular Rich20Something column on *Huffington Post* and contributes regularly to other national publications, including *TIME* magazine, *Fortune, Entrepreneur, Business Insider,* Fox News, and Yahoo Finance. He lives in Los Angeles, California.